The Question of All Questions

The Question of All Questions

Where Did We Come From and Where Are We Going?

What Water Will We Drink and What Air Will We Breathe 200 Years from Now?

A Road Map for Building a More Civilized Society

Frank Stronach

To order additional copies of this book, contact:
Xlibris
1-888-795-4274
www.Xlibris.com
Orders@Xlibris.com
770506

Pegasus and Dragon, shown here in this spectacular bronze monument, are eternal symbols of light and darkness, creation and destruction, good and evil. The monument, located next to Gulfstream Park in Florida, is both a tribute to the majestic horse and a representation of the struggle between the forces of good and evil—forces that have shaped human history and continue to influence our own personal lives and the lives of those around us each and every day. The timeless themes and issues symbolized by the monument are reflected in this book.

Acknowledgments

I wish to thank Mark Kara for the cover design and for his artistic input in the creation of the *Pegasus and Dragon* statue, as well as Paul Pivato for his assistance with the writing of this book.

One of the World's Most Innovative Business Leaders Shares His Passion, Wisdom and Insight

Frank Stronach is the founder and Honorary Chairman of Magna International Inc., a leading global auto-parts supplier he started in a small garage that today employs more than 150,000 people, as well as the founder and Honorary Chairman of The Stronach Group, North America's leading Thoroughbred racetrack operator and one of the world's largest suppliers of pari-mutuel wagering systems, technologies and services. He is also one of the world's leading Thoroughbred racehorse owners and breeders. He has served on a wide range of corporate, government and university boards and is the recipient of numerous honorary degrees and awards for his achievements in business and philanthropy. He has been a strong advocate over the years for the right of employees to share in the profits they help produce and the profit-sharing formula he established at Magna International Inc. is widely credited as one of the key reasons for that company's growth and success.

"As the founder of Magna International Inc., I've built hundreds of factories employing more than 150,000 people in 30 different countries. So over the course of my career, I have gotten to know the hopes and dreams of people from all over the world. People everywhere share the same desire for freedom and the opportunity to build a better life for themselves and their families. My focus in writing this book was to put forward ways in which we could create a more civilized society by preventing war and eliminating poverty, while also improving the economy in order to raise the living standards of people everywhere around the world."

- Frank Stronach

To my wife, Elfriede; my children, Belinda and Andrew; and my grandchildren, Frank, Nikki, and Selena. It is my sincere wish that they will continue to donate their time and talents in order to help build a better world.

Reflections on Building a Better Society

Focus on the day, to stay alive, to survive. But leave the door open for tomorrow, to follow your dreams. And as you follow your dreams, always be guided by your conscience.

Our conscience is a reflection of our soul. And it is our soul which lives continuously and unceasingly in search of the truth, in search of equilibrium. It seeks to serve others and is the ultimate expression of our humanity. Our soul is embedded in our children and in our grandchildren, and it shapes and guides their future. This is a never-ending process—the process to find the road to happiness for all people and to live in harmony with the laws of the universe.

It is human nature to pass judgement on our parents and their generation for failing to leave behind a more perfect world. But families are the foundation of a society. Families are the living links between the past and the future, between the generations that came before us and those yet to be born. That is why it is vital that families live together in love and harmony, and pass along, from one generation to the next, the task of building a better world.

Contents

"Unfortunately, the history of humankind has always been, and still is, dominated by the Golden Rule: the man who has the gold makes the rules. I would never want anyone to dominate me or my children, and if I feel that strongly, then I should never expect to be able to dominate anyone else. So the challenge we as a society face is this: we must find a way to dismantle the chains of domination—not via a destructive revolution, but via a revolution of the mind."

"The problem with Free Enterprise is that more and more capital is held by fewer and fewer people, and as a result, there are fewer and fewer capitalists. But in nature, whenever a species does not reproduce itself, another species will take over. That is why I believe that Free Enterprise can only survive if workers are given the opportunity to participate in wealth creation. In plain English, workers must have the opportunity to become capitalists—to accumulate capital by sharing in the profits they help produce."

Preface

"Free Enterprise made America great, and we must do everything possible to preserve the Free Enterprise system because it is the foundation of a free society."

One of the great things about getting older is that I have more time to count my blessings and to reflect on life. There are so many eternal questions to ponder, but perhaps the greatest is: where did we come from, and where are we going? What lies beyond our galaxy? What water will we drink, what food will we eat, and what air will we breathe two hundred years from now? Two hundred years is not far away—it is mere seconds when measured against the span of time that life has existed on Earth.

Our home, the planet Earth, is a relatively small piece of real estate, with more and more people born every year. Approximately nine billion people live on our planet today, and in all likelihood, there will be around twenty billion people two hundred years from now. But if we continue to have the same lifestyle and if we continue to consume natural resources at the rate we do today, the planet Earth will not be able to sustain all those billions of people. In this book, I attempt to address a number of the problems facing our world today. I have always been a great believer that if you identify a problem, you need to bring forward a solution, even if it exposes you to criticism. After all, the turtle only makes progress when it sticks its neck out.

Through hard work, drive, and determination, I have had the good fortune to accomplish great things and to live an extraordinary life. I am a toolmaker by trade. In 1957, I rented a small garage, bought a few old used machines, and went hustling for business. I was full of confidence when I walked into factories and businesses and pitched my skills and services. I would tell my prospective clients that if I could not solve their problems, they would not have to pay me. I picked up some orders fairly quickly, and after one month, I hired an employee. After one year, I had about ten employees. Then I opened a new factory and soon after, another, until I got to the point several decades later when I was opening a new factory somewhere around the world every month.

Sixty years later, the company I built from scratch has 163,000 employees and approximately $35 billion in annual sales. The company I founded is Magna International, one of the world's largest auto-parts makers, recognized worldwide for its development of highly advanced automotive technologies. Nearly every car and truck on the road today features high-quality parts produced by Magna.

By the time I retired from Magna, we had approximately four hundred factories and product R&D centers operating in thirty different countries. When I was the CEO, I made it a point to be involved in a wide range of social and commercial activities. I have been on the board of directors of numerous universities, hospitals, banks, and charitable organizations and was a member of the corporate governance board of the NASDAQ Stock Market. Later in my career, I became the leader of a national political party and an elected Member of Parliament in Austria, and during that time, I gained incredible insights into how democratic systems of government operate—their inner workings and their built-in flaws. I witnessed firsthand how they function, and I learned how they can be improved.

Life has been incredibly good to me. I've met kings and queens, presidents and prime ministers, the rich and the famous, a lot of colourful characters and plenty of decent, down-to-earth people. Even though I have experienced the lowest of the lows and the highest of the highs, it is the hardships I have endured that have made me the person I am today and taught me the business lessons that helped me grow Magna into an auto-parts empire. I have lived under the boot of two of the most brutal regimes the world has ever seen— all within the span of just a few years. I have known hunger and hardship. I've been fired and laid off and discriminated against. All these experiences have left deep impressions.

Over the course of my career, I have spent many decades living and working here in the USA. I value the principles of freedom that America stands for, and I admire the entrepreneurial, can-do spirit of Americans. **I believe that America is the last country in the world where Free Enterprise may have a chance to survive.** Free Enterprise made America great, and we must do everything possible to preserve the Free Enterprise system because it is the foundation of a free society. I believe the best way to do this is by giving employees the opportunity to participate in the creation of wealth through profit sharing.

In the past several decades, we've witnessed a growing trend in America toward the adoption of socialistic policies—policies that are focused on the *distribution* of wealth rather than the *creation* of wealth. I've seen firsthand how Europe has travelled far down the road toward socialism, and the same sort of detrimental policies that have become entrenched in Europe are gaining ground in the USA. As a result, I believe we've reached a dangerous tipping point where more and more people are taking out of our economy and fewer and fewer people are contributing to it, with a growing number of Americans becoming dependent on government handouts for their survival.

Business is largely to blame because it has failed to engage employees by making them partners in productivity and profits. In the final analysis, **if workers** don't feel that they are getting a fair slice of the economic pie, then they will be tempted to support government wealth redistribution policies, and we, as a society, will slide further toward a socialistic system.

America is also confronted by a number of other fundamental economic problems. We are increasingly becoming a financial economy instead of a real economy—one that makes products. You can see how far we have drifted away from a real economy by walking down the aisles of a major department store and observing that hardly any of the products on the shelves are made in North America or Europe. One of the main reasons for this is that companies in the West are actually rewarded by our tax system for closing factories and shifting their manufacturing to Asia and other low-cost regions. It should be the other way around: companies that invest their profits in America should be rewarded by receiving a reduction in taxes.

In addition, the current tax structure is not conducive to manufacturing. When you look around, whenever new buildings are springing up, they are seldom factories anymore; increasingly, they are warehouses for imported products made in Asia. **When a country imports more and more and exports less and less, the economy will inevitably deteriorate**, causing rising unemployment.

That is why I believe that Free Enterprise can only survive if workers are given the opportunity to participate in wealth creation. In plain English, **workers must have the opportunity to become capitalists—to accumulate capital by receiving a share of the profits they help produce.**

The core principle of Free Enterprise is the creation of wealth, also known as capital. This is the reason why Free Enterprise is also commonly referred to as capitalism or the capitalist system. Unfortunately, more and more capital today is held by fewer people. In other words, there are fewer and fewer capitalists. And in nature, whenever a species does not reproduce itself, another species will take over. In order for Free Enterprise to survive, therefore, we must broaden our understanding of how wealth is created and how that wealth is distributed.

The well-being of a country depends on the health of its economic fabric. Businesses are the weavers of that fabric. Business is driven by three forces: smart managers, motivated employees, and investors. All three forces have a moral right to some of the profits the business generates. As a general guideline, employees would share 20 percent of the profits. Management would get 10 percent. Investors would receive 20 percent, and the remaining 50 percent would stay in the business for investments as well as product research and development in order to be competitive in the future. **Via profit sharing, workers would be given the opportunity to accumulate capital or, in other words, to become capitalists.**

We have to realize that the democratic system within a Free Enterprise society is constituency-driven. In practical terms, this means that if there are fewer capitalists and if the gap between the wealthy and the workers continues to grow larger, then political parties will cater to the masses by promising wealth redistribution measures and socialistic programs. The end result is that a Free Enterprise society gets slowly pulled toward a socialistic system.

Over the years, I built many factories in Europe and have spent a fair amount of time there managing our business operations. I noted earlier how socialism has become deeply entrenched throughout Europe. I do not say that in a cynical way because I come from a working-class family and my father was a labor activist. But I do not believe that socialism can raise living standards or eliminate poverty. **Socialistic philosophies are based on the distribution of wealth rather than the creation of wealth.** What socialism fails to account for is that we must first create wealth before we can distribute it.

In nearly every instance where socialism has been adopted, the country has ended up being driven into economic ruin. A typical example of this was East

Germany. After World War II, Germany was split into two countries—West Germany, which operated under Free Enterprise principles, and East Germany, which operated under socialist and communist philosophies. After four decades under communist rule, East Germany's infrastructure began to crumble, the economy collapsed, and the country could no longer feed itself. We are seeing the same tragic course of events taking place today in Venezuela, another country that embraced socialism.

But how does our society preserve not only Free Enterprise but the rights and freedoms on which it is built? I believe one way to do this is to establish a national values program that is taught in every school in America from the first grade until the end of high school. Naturally, the teaching of these values would be very simple and rudimentary in the younger grades and then become more in-depth as students matured.

The values or principles taught in this program would include many of the freedoms enshrined in the US Bill of Rights—everything from the freedom of expression and the freedom of religion to the freedom of assembly, which gives people the right to form political parties and advocacy groups. But the national values program would also focus on other freedoms as well, such as the freedom to choose your own road to happiness, and Free Enterprise itself, because America is the last country in the world where the Free Enterprise system may have a chance to survive. **Free Enterprise is one of the bedrock principles of our society; without Free Enterprise, there can be no free society.**

I believe we have many excellent teachers in schools across America. I've known many teachers in my life, and I've found most of them to be noble-minded. But when it comes to teaching about business, many teachers often highlight the wrongdoings that businesses sometimes commit—everything from corporate fraud to the exploitation of child labor. And it's only right that students should be made aware of these matters.

But unfortunately, not enough is done to stress how important business is to the functioning of our society. Profit should not be a dirty word. **If a company does not make a profit, it is no good to anyone: not to its shareholders and owners, not to its employees, and not to society at large.** When businesses fail, society fails too. There is greater unemployment, which in turn creates a lot of social hardship, and living standards begin to erode. In the final analysis, **if the economy doesn't function, nothing else will.**

Besides highlighting the many freedoms discussed above and the importance of the economy, the national values program should also include awareness about the environment and how truly fragile it is. The environment supports all life on our planet and gives us the food we need to eat in order to live.

And in the context of the food we produce and consume, students need to be taught to eat healthy, natural foods. When I was a kid, we never heard of children having allergies, and now, it's the other way around: more and more children have food allergies of one kind or another. But teaching our children about the importance of eating natural chemical-free foods will go a long way to creating a healthier society.

Health statistics show a tremendous increase in illnesses among all Americans of every demographic. **On top of that, the USA spends double what all other developed countries spend per capita on health care.** In my own analysis of why American health costs are so high, I came to the conclusion that one key factor for the rise in illness is the fact that most of the foods we eat contain a lot of chemicals. Americans are ingesting millions and millions of pounds of chemicals, insecticides, pesticides, and fertilizers in their food each year.

We are becoming a sicker and sicker society, and health-care spending is on track to becoming the single biggest budget expenditure, surpassing even military spending. The spin-off effect of increased rates of illness and premature death in America will ripple throughout the economy, lowering productivity and forcing taxes to climb in order to pay for the increased costs associated with health care. I discuss how we can bring down costs while enhancing health care and improving access in chapter 20.

A national values program would go a long way to bolstering our education system. But there is still much more we can do. The basic building blocks of our education system should also include greater learning in regard to the technical trades that make our society function—everything from electricians and plumbers to carpenters and mechanics.

It's critical that our youth are exposed to these trades, many of which will be in great demand in the decade ahead. When I give lectures at universities, **I always tell the students that success in life can only be measured by the degree of happiness you attain**. At the same time, I also tell them that, based on my own experience, it's a lot easier to be happy if you have money. And when students ask how to go about making money, I always say that they need to be exposed to many career options; they need to gain some hands-on learning out in the real world. I conclude by saying that if they find a job or trade that they enjoy, then there's a strong chance that they will be good at their job, and if they put in extra effort, they could eventually become one of the very best in their chosen field. Whether it's business or some other field of endeavor, when you are one of the best, money will be a natural by-product of that success. The need for more trade apprenticeship learning is one of a broad range of educational reforms we need to undertake which I discuss in chapter 19.

One of the great dangers of any democratic society is the enormous buildup of bureaucracy. I remember the time when computers first came on the market. Businesses were told that a computer could do the work of one entire floor of employees in a typical office building. Now, decades later, I see ten to twenty times more high-rise office buildings, staffed by employees who are spending a large portion of their time ensuring that the business is complying with increased government regulations. The reality is **the harder a bureaucrat works, the more bureaucrats he or she will create.** It is why the buildup of bureaucracy continues year after year.

As a society, we are increasingly losing sight of the truth that **governments cannot give you anything unless they take it from you in the first place**, and in that process, they end up wasting a lot of the money they take. Of course, we require laws to protect the environment and to safeguard human health. But most of the mountain of government rules and regulations that have been created over the years can be simplified, streamlined, and made less complicated.

We need to begin reducing the massive size of government and reining in out-of-control government spending. I believe we can do this by creating a task force dedicated to reducing the amount of laws and regulations that govern virtually every aspect of our life and work. The task force should enlist bureaucrats themselves in the process of identifying government duplication and overlap and providing them with generous bonuses and incentives for bringing forward recommendations that lead to savings. I discuss how we can do this in chapters 17 and 18.

The tax system has the greatest bearing on the health of the economy. But the tax system today is so complex and murky that it is hindering economic growth and imposing a massive burden on business and taxpayers. **Consider this: in 1913, the entire extent of US tax law was twenty-seven pages. Today, just more than a century later, the US federal tax code is close to seventy-five thousand pages.**

According to estimates published in 2016 from the Office of Information and Regulatory Affairs, Americans spend more than 8.9 billion hours per year complying with IRS tax filing—the equivalent of one year's work for 4.3 million full-time workers. The Tax Foundation, an independent tax policy institute, estimates that the growing amount of time needed to comply with the tax code translates into more than $400 billion in lost productivity annually.

In the 1980s, when US President Ronald Reagan tried to show how ridiculously convoluted the US tax code was, he often cited the following example from Section 509(a):

> **For purposes of paragraph (3), an organization described in paragraph (2) shall be deemed to include an organization described in section 501(c)(4), (5), or (6) which would be described in paragraph (2) if it were an organization described in section 501(c)(3).**

Section 509(a) remains unchanged in the tax code to this day, together with thousands of new and equally impossible-to-understand regulations that have been added in the years since then.

The only people who are benefitting from the tax system are the tax lawyers and tax specialists who make a lucrative wage deciphering our incredibly complex tax laws for their clients. These experts are often the same people who helped write the convoluted tax laws. This constitutes a clear conflict of interest, and it is astonishing there has not been a greater public outcry about this abuse of the tax system.

We need a system that is simple and clear-cut. And although I would not recommend that we change the tax system overnight, there are a number of steps we could take, including eliminating personal income tax and replacing it with a straightforward consumption tax and eliminating corporate tax and replacing it with an easy-to-calculate sales tax. I show how we can reform taxes in chapter 14.

I believe the American Constitution is still the best of all the countries in the world. Drafted by the Founding Fathers, who years earlier in the Declaration of Independence had proclaimed the aspirations of humans everywhere—*"life, liberty, and the pursuit of happiness"*—the US Constitution laid the foundation for a democratic system of government that guarantees every American citizen more rights and freedoms than any nation on Earth.

But over time, our system of democracy has become overly politicized, and deeply entrenched parties, together with a professional class of politicians, have gotten a stranglehold on the way our democracy functions, creating deadlock and obstruction. This was never the intent of the original spirit of the Constitution, and **America's first president, George Washington, warned the country in his farewell address to prevent partisan politics from taking over the Senate and House of Representatives**.

There is a simple way that we can solve the problem of partisan politics—a solution that would restore democratic control to the people who elect their government representatives. I discuss that solution in greater detail in chapter 16.

The primary purpose for me in writing this book was to provide a road map for an ideal society. And I believe that **America represents the world's best chance to build an ideal society**. But America must first overcome a major problem, one that continues to grow like a cancer: poverty in our inner cities. Everything we have tried for the past half century has not worked. In chapter 22, I propose a unique solution: urban farming. I believe it would not only provide meaningful jobs but would restore pride and hope in the poverty-stricken neighborhoods of our major cities.

The many reforms proposed in this book can only exist in an environment where there is harmony. Without peace, all the key pillars of society would be in a constant state of turmoil and disruption. And the reality of today's world is that peace depends upon the mutual respect and cooperation of the globe's three superpowers: America, Russia, and China. I discuss some ideas on how we can reduce tensions between the world's three superpowers in chapter 25.

In the chapters that follow, I analyze the various segments of society, and I bring forward some solutions.

Many of them are common-sense solutions. Some of them are innovative. All of them are practical and easy to implement. They are clear-cut and straightforward ideas that any person can understand.

There are many think tanks in the world—institutes filled with experts who study and analyze a wide range of topics from social and political policy to economics. They are always thinking but never doing. What we need are more "do tanks"—organizations and individuals who are constantly looking for new and innovative ways to turn practical, common-sense thinking into effective action.

I'm a great believer in identifying problems and then taking action to solve them. Sometimes, however, the solution is easier to arrive at than identifying the problem in the first place. **If things don't function properly, be it in your personal life, in your business, or in your country, you should know that you've got a problem. If you don't know that you've got a problem, then you've really got a problem**. And problems are like cancer: if left unattended, they will grow.

I would never pretend to have all the answers or that my solutions are the only solutions. On the contrary, what I hope to do is to spark dialogue and discussion, realizing that the search for solutions to make this world a better place is an ongoing process.

The further you look back in history, the further you can see the future. Most people are so preoccupied with meeting the challenges of everyday life that they have very little time to reflect. Young people hardly ever look back—they only see the future. It has always been this way. Also, when people start their own businesses, they are so engaged in running the business that they hardly have any time to do anything else. I know this from personal experience.

I've been very blessed. I'm eighty-five years young. I'm very healthy and fit, and I'm still involved in business. But I have slowed down, and now I find that I have more time to stop and smell the roses. At the same time, though, my mind still races at a hundred miles per hour. And I have been heavily preoccupied more recently with the question: what is the purpose of life?

We humans have been bestowed with extraordinary senses, a conscience, a soul, and the ability to judge between good and bad. I do not believe that a sophisticated species like *Homo sapiens* evolved from the smallest of organisms over billions of years of evolution. I believe there are other forces in the universe which we humans will never understand.

But nevertheless, I believe in something good. And the world's great religions are also based on this same foundation of goodness. My philosophy in life is that everyone should find their own road to happiness without preventing others from doing the same. And I believe that we must let everyone find their own road to God. Because of those deeply held convictions, I believe that the purpose of life is that we as a people should try each and every day, according to our means and abilities, to make a contribution, however small, to making this a better world.

The world has always been influenced by the spirit of goodness and the spirit of evil. That is one of the reasons why I built a massive bronze monument in Florida called *Pegasus and Dragon*. The sculpture strikingly portrays the bronze winged stallion of Greek legend in combat with a fire-spewing dragon. The monument not only honors the horse for its service to mankind, but it is also meant to provoke the mind and nourish the soul of anyone who stands before it.

The monument is part myth and part fantasy, a symbol of the cosmic struggle that has defined our history and shapes our future: the clash between the forces of good and evil, creation and destruction, light and darkness. Many of the problems we face today are still rooted in that age-old conflict. And each of us must also struggle, in our own personal lives, with doing what is good and right or doing harm to our planet and to others.

For me, the monument became a catalyst for thinking about where we came from and where we are headed.

It made me think about our human journey on this planet, about our past that stretches back to prehistoric times, and about our future. The more involved I became in the design and construction of this epic statue, the more deeply entwined I became in the questions and mysteries it posed. What do the ancient myths and sagas and scriptures teach us about our origins and our nature?

There are many questions that we will never know the answer to. We are constrained by the limits of our human intelligence—there is only so much we can know and only so much we can discover, despite our unquenchable thirst to know more about every aspect of life.

So my questioning and fascination with these timeless truths led me to think about the ideal society. Can we build such a society, and if so, how do we get there?

Despite the many challenges we face today, from war and poverty to oppression and environmental destruction, I believe it is possible to build the ideal society—a society that provides equality and opportunity for all, that upholds democratic rights and freedoms, a society where no one goes hungry and everyone has access to shelter and health care.

After a long and successful career, I would like to share my knowledge and experience in the pursuit of building a better world. This book is the result of that sincere desire to give back to society.

In the pages that follow, I outline some of the building blocks of an ideal society—a free and healthy and economically prosperous society that allows every individual the opportunity to pursue his or her own road to happiness. If implemented, I believe we could get off the destructive path we are on—one headed toward intensified conflict and war, growing poverty and environmental destruction. I believe we would instead be able to build the framework of a better world and a much more prosperous future for our children and our grandchildren.

Frank Stronach
Adena Farms
Ocala, Florida

Chapter 1

Introduction

"We are entering a perilous time in human history—a period where a wrong turn could lead to the collapse of civilization as we know it and the destruction of our planet. But at the same time, the human spirit possesses incredibly positive energy and is capable of leading humanity to a higher plateau."

Driving along US 1, the highway that hugs the Atlantic coast of Florida, you suddenly see it in the distance, rising majestically above the swaying palm trees. Standing ten stories tall and sheathed in dazzling bronze, it is the world's largest horse sculpture, *Pegasus and Dragon.*

It is unlike anything on earth. It sits near the entranceway to Gulfstream Park in Hallandale, Florida, a now-iconic monument that pays homage to the courage, speed, and power of the horse. One of the greatest bronze statues ever made, it is more than 100 feet tall and weighs 715 tons. The monument features Pegasus, the winged horse of Greek mythology, standing triumphantly over a fallen dragon.

The idea to build the world's greatest horse statue first came to me about ten years ago when we launched a massive redevelopment of Gulfstream Park. We wanted to remake Gulfstream, one of the premier horse-racing destinations in North America, into a bold prototype for the future of the American horse-racing industry—an entertainment destination center in the Sunshine State complete with a casino with 850 slot machines and high-stakes poker tables, luxury suite skyboxes, live shows, upscale shopping and dining, and ocean-view condo developments.

We wanted to bring a touch of Vegas to the racetrack. But we also wanted to bring a bit of Disney as well by creating a horse-related entertainment theme park right next to the racetrack that would draw tourists from across America and around the world to the heart of Florida's ocean playground.

That's when I first began thinking about a giant horse sculpture as the possible centerpiece of the theme park—something that would be spectacular, enduring, and inspirational. I wanted to honor the great contributions that horses have made to human civilization throughout history—everything from the horse and chariots of ancient Rome to the cowboys and horses that opened up the American West.

But for my sculpture, I didn't want just a regular horse—I wanted something fantastical, something at once heroic and epic. Working together with American artist Mark Kara five years ago, I drafted a rough sketch of Pegasus, the celebrated horse of Greek mythology, standing victoriously over a vanquished dragon. From those early sketches, we began producing small-scale versions in clay and plaster of what the sculpture would look like once complete.

I was repeatedly told that a sculpture of the size I envisioned—one that surpasses the Statue of Liberty in weight, size, and complexity—would be virtually impossible to create. But we persevered, and in the end, we completed *Pegasus and Dragon*, a monument coated in precious metal that will stand the test of time.

Located on the north side of Gulfstream Park, the towering sculpture is a marvel of modern-day engineering. Under the direction of the renowned century-old German art foundry Strassacker, the frame of the sculpture was fabricated in Germany and built by more than 500 workers, then shipped to Gulfstream as 4,750 pieces of steel and 1,250 bronze sections. The sculpture is supported by a highly complex internal steel skeleton with massive steel girders anchored deeply into the rock formations below and is designed to withstand hurricane-force winds. The steel skeleton itself was assembled with 18,000 gigantic bolts measuring two inches in diameter, the thickness of a sledgehammer. The bronze sections were then placed over the steel skeleton and welded together.

The sculpture's outer bronze layer, fastened to the steel structure in sections measuring six feet by nine feet, weighs more than half a million pounds and was fitted together with microscopic precision. The entire bronze surface of the sculpture was then sandblasted, cleaned, and given a patina application that involved heating each section with a gas torch to create an oxidation process, giving the metal its distinguished color.

The journey we embarked on in designing and building the statue was as epic as the monument itself, involving hundreds of workers, up to seventy sculptors, some of the world's greatest artists and craftsmen and welders, and a voyage across the seas in twenty-five ocean-freight containers, with each container approximately forty-five feet in length and ten feet tall, carrying upwards of fifty thousand pounds. To make the various sections of the statue, we used numerous production methods, including pouring liquid bronze into sand molds at 2,000 degrees Fahrenheit, the same temperature as volcanic lava.

I personally poured a lot of time and effort into the statue. And to this day, people ask me why I went to such great lengths to erect the *Pegasus and Dragon* statue.

First and foremost, I wanted to create something enormously entertaining and spectacular. I wanted to create a racetrack that the whole family could go to, with an entertainment theme park filled with horse-related attractions.

But I also wanted to create a monument in dedication to the horse and the vital role they have played throughout the history of human civilization. Around the turn of the last century, before the introduction of the automobile, most Americans lived on farms, and on those farms, most people owned horses. Horses were an integral part of life, and there was a much greater connection between horses and people. People valued horses; people loved them. But in today's mechanized world, there are fewer and fewer horses. The bond between horses and humans has begun to fade away.

Since its grand unveiling in 2016, the majestic *Pegasus and Dragon* sculpture has already become a major Florida landmark. It will greet visitors to Gulfstream Park for generations to come and will serve as a beacon for one of the Sunshine State's most celebrated entertainment destinations.

But *Pegasus and Dragon* is more than a modern-day monument to the horse—it's also a classic symbol of the struggle between good and evil, a struggle that is as old as humanity itself. Pegasus is a symbol of goodness, and it has nobility and strength that overcame the dragon, the age-old embodiment of evil. Who among us, young or old, doesn't admire the grace and power of the horse? Who isn't fascinated by dragons? And who doesn't long for the triumph of good over evil? Pegasus represents the qualities we admire and esteem—everything from beauty and strength to speed and agility. The fire-spitting dragon, meanwhile, epitomizes the very worst qualities within us: fear, anger, malice, and wanton destruction.

These mythological creatures will be forever captivating to people of all countries, creeds, and cultures. And their symbolic struggle—the timeless struggle between good and evil, creation and destruction—will remain as relevant centuries from now as it is today.

The eternal conflict between good and evil is not only the central theme that runs through the teachings of the world's great religions and the classic works of literature, it's also a never-ending struggle that has guided the destiny of human civilization. Within the past century alone, humanity has suffered genocide, oppression, and death caused by weapons of mass destruction. And yet despite this unrelenting brutality and evil, there still burns within the human heart a yearning to build a better world and an enduring belief that goodness can triumph over evil.

Against the backdrop of the struggle between good and evil lie a number of other contests that continue to shape societies and delineate the arc of human history: the fight between freedom and oppression, the struggle between individualism and collectivism, and the clash between democracy and totalitarianism. And buried deeper within these larger struggles are other age-old dualities: creation versus destruction, knowledge versus ignorance, health versus sickness, and the desire to preserve what is natural in a world that is increasingly artificial. These eternal conflicts and tensions lie at the heart of our collective past and our shared destiny.

As a young child, I saw human brutality in the form of fascism, first under the boot of the Nazis and then under the Soviet Communists. Even though I was young, I would ask myself: What makes people act this way? Why do people choose to oppress and harm their fellow humans? Is this our natural instinct or is this behavior instilled in us by those who want to control and conquer? People can be malicious and consumed by hatred. And yet people can also be selfless, noble, and good. This duality or syndrome that is rooted deep within our nature has perplexed the human mind since time immemorial, and it is captured and frozen forever in the struggle between the mythological creatures in *Pegasus and Dragon*.

This book explores these timeless struggles and charts a pathway to a better world. **If we don't have a concept of an ideal society, then we can't put together the building blocks needed to make it a reality.** Most importantly, this book shows how human civilization stands today at a crossroads, and it gives a broad outline of the steps we need to take in order to get to the next plateau in our evolution. We are entering a perilous time in human history—a period where a wrong turn could lead to the collapse of civilization as we know it and the destruction of our planet. But at the same time, the human spirit possesses incredibly positive energy and is capable of leading humanity to a higher plateau.

This book seeks to inspire individuals to reach for ever greater heights of human achievement and success. It challenges us to seek out what is good and to overcome that which is evil. And it calls on all of us to ensure that good will ultimately prevail.

Chapter 2

The Origins of the Universe: Our Search for Meaning

"Nature always seeks equilibrium and balance, and the laws of nature are much stronger than any man-made laws."

When we look up at the starry skies at night, when we stare at the vast expanse of the Milky Way galaxy and beyond, many of us are overcome with a sense of awe and wonder about life's many mysteries. We wonder: Where did we come from? Where are we going? Is there life beyond our planet? Will we unravel some of the mysteries of the universe when we are able one day to journey through space to other planets in far-off galaxies? Although we may never know with certainty the answers to these and many other questions, we do know this: we have within our grasp the power to improve the world we live in.

The origins and extent of the universe will always be shrouded in mystery, with the possibility of no beginning and no end. Ultimately, I believe it boils down to belief—a belief in a good and all-powerful creator or God or a belief that the universe came about because of trillions of interconnected evolutionary processes over billions of years. It is inconceivable to me that the human species evolved from a microscopic cell or organism, even over hundreds of millions of years of evolution. And if we are the end result of evolution, does it mean that we do not possess a conscience or a soul that lives on for all eternity? Or does it mean that when we die, we simply rot in the earth like a worm, our brief existence on this Earth buried forever? And then there is the question of all questions: if God does in fact exist, who created God?

In the end, however, I truly believe that we will never find with complete and final certainty the answer to the questions about where we came from and how we got here. We will never totally understand the natural laws of the universe that govern our existence and the existence of all life.

In addition to the mystery about God and eternity, there are many other questions about the world we live in that we wrestle with over the course of our lives. For example: is the universe good and noble, or is it cruel and indifferent? It's a question we've contemplated ever since humankind first walked the earth. Undeniably, we experience sudden and sometimes catastrophic natural disasters—everything from earthquakes and tornadoes to torrential floods and fires—that kill people and destroy homes and villages. And every day, we read about personal tragedies that strike from time to time: horrible car crashes, a drowning at the beach or in a backyard pool, random acts of terror on the subway or train. On the whole, though, I believe there are more good events that happen in life than bad ones and that we are more often than not the authors of our own misfortune.

It is also undeniable that some people are more blessed than others. They are born in better health or grow up in better circumstances and surroundings. And it's likewise true that people's lives can be cut short or diminished through no fault of their own—for example, a child who is stricken by a crippling disease or a teenager who develops an incurable cancer. And yet despite all these many afflictions, hardships, and misfortunes, I still hold to the view that the world is on the whole more good than bad. I choose to believe in something good. Life would lose its meaning and become unbearable if we did not believe in and embrace the concept of goodness, if we did not strive for what is good.

Over the last several thousand years, various religions have risen and spread throughout different regions of the world, and people have built glorified temples and places of worship in the name of these religions, including Christianity, Islam, Buddhism, Judaism, and Hinduism. When you take a closer look at many of these religions, you see that they share several features in common: they uphold and teach a code of values and morals, they believe in a superior being or God, they believe in the existence of an eternal soul, and they all preach about the pursuit of goodness.

In addition, countless stories, fables, and scriptures have been written in regard to the eternal conflict and tension that exists between God and the devil, good and evil, heaven and hell. At the same time, all these religions also teach about the eternal punishment and everlasting rewards—heaven or hell, paradise or damnation—that await people based on their behavior here on Earth.

I believe that people are born with the instinct to strive for goodness, and the one great hope that we all have and hold on to is that there is more good in this world than bad. In the end, human life is sustained and uplifted by an ever-present hope—hope that we can not only survive the many accidents and disasters that befall us but create a better world and a better future. Humans have the will, the spirit, and the brain power to elevate humanity to a higher plateau, to a place where we can attain greater harmony and balance. In short, we have within us the ability to create an ideal society.

If we look around us at all the creatures on this planet—everything from the smallest bacteria to the insects and birds and mammals—it seems that they all have a purpose in this world. Birds and bees help pollinate our flowers and trees. Worms help aerate the soil. Plankton keep the oceans clean, provide abundant food to fish and mammals that live in the water, and give the Earth much of the oxygen that we breathe.

And so it goes for thousands of other different species of plant and animal life. In some cases, we're not able to fully determine what role an organism or animal plays in the grand scheme of the universe, but we do know there is a great chance that this life form, no matter how small and primitive or how big and sophisticated, has been created with a purpose in mind and has a role to play in the ebb and flow of life on Earth.

But what about us? What is our purpose in life? What role do we play? I believe we have been put on this planet to make it even better, to add to the glorious creation that the universe has bestowed upon us. Mother Nature gives us lush forests and fields, but among all the animals on Earth, it is only we humans who can divert the course of a river to bring water where it never flowed before or make once-arid deserts blossom and bloom. I also believe that we are the custodians of this beautiful blue planet on the outer edge of the Milky Way. We have been given the task of caring for and bettering the world we live in, and we are failing to live up to our obligations.

While we may never know the origins of the universe or even the meaning of life, we do know that the universe is predicated on balance—the balance between day and night, heat and cold, wet and dry. It is the balance captured in the ancient Tao symbol of yin and yang, the striking image of opposite forces forever intertwined and interconnected. Balance brings symmetry, order, and peace. But imbalance always leads to disparity and disorder.

One of the supreme laws of nature that governs the universe is the constant striving to attain balance. It is an impulse that flows through all creation, all life. The question that we must ask ourselves, therefore, is this: can humanity find a more perfect balance in order to minimize the conflict and chaos that increasingly have come to characterize our world? As individuals, we seek balance in all aspects of our lives. For me personally, balance is the most important word in my vocabulary. But that same search for balance should guide the functioning of our societies, our governments, and our economies. Attaining greater balance in human affairs will solve many of the problems that weigh down our world. Greater balance, for example, will lead to less disparity in wealth, less war and conflict, and less poverty. The greater the fluctuation or imbalance that exists, the more humankind will suffer.

Nature always seeks equilibrium and balance, and the laws of nature are much stronger than any man-made laws. But at the same time, nature can also be cruel: from earthquakes and tornadoes to gigantic forest fires and torrential floods, the forces of nature can bring about the deaths of many innocent lives. This destructive force of nature can seem malicious or even meaningless, but at the same time, it is undeniably a part of the balance of nature. Forest fires, for example, cause massive devastation, burning down everything in their path, but from the ashes comes new growth and new creation.

Earlier, I noted that we were often the cause of the many problems that derail and destroy our peace and prosperity. The truth is, without balance, we will encounter more disasters, more upheaval, more war, and more environmental degradation. But the closer we can come to achieving balance, the greater the likelihood that we will be able to establish an ideal society. Balance is the key. But it is a never-ending quest. In the end, any balance we achieve will be extremely fragile, and without constant vigilance and effort on our part, that balance would begin to slip away and become undone.

In the previous chapter, I explained why I chose two mythological creatures—Pegasus and the Dragon—to symbolize the struggle between good and evil, light and darkness, and the eternal quest to seek balance between the conflicting and sometimes opposite forces within the universe. The struggle between these two mythic creatures and opposing forces of nature encapsulates for me the struggle we face as humans, both within our own personal lives as well as within the broader context of the societies and worlds we create.

The ancient Greeks named one of the greatest constellations in the cosmos after Pegasus. And today, many thousands of years later, when we look up into the northern hemisphere at night, we can make out the Pegasus constellation, one of the largest in the celestial sky. According to Greek mythology, Zeus placed Pegasus there after he returned to Mount Olympus from Earth—perhaps in tribute to the loyal friend of humankind or perhaps as a reminder to us to rein in our human pride and arrogance.

According to the greatest of all the Pegasus myths, the human warrior Bellerophon was able to tame Pegasus and mount his back to go into battle against the Chimaera, a fire-breathing monster much like the dragon. After defeating the Chimaera, Bellerophon became so swollen with pride and self-importance that he attempted to fly Pegasus to Olympus so he could live among the gods. However, on his journey to the heavens, he fell off the horse and tumbled back to Earth. Perhaps we are more like Bellerophon than we imagine, and perhaps we too need reminding that we are not as godlike as we sometimes suppose and in fact may be heading for a fall. Either way, these myths live on from generation to generation because they contain within them certain timeless truths about our nature and the human condition.

We are a unique species: *Homo sapiens*, Latin for "wise man." Among all the animals, we alone have been gifted with extraordinary intelligence and the capability to create a perfect world—a world without war and poverty, a world where people respect and love each other and live together in harmony. But at the same time, we also wield the power to wipe out and extinguish all life on planet Earth.

All around us, day after day, more and more, there are a growing number of signs that we are crossing a line we may never be able to come back from—whether it's poisoning our air, water, and food with chemicals and toxins, or driving hundreds of species to the brink of extinction while destroying their habitats, or amassing nuclear weapons of annihilation. We are racing down the road that leads to the destruction of the Earth.

The crucial question humankind faces today is this: will our future be a paradise on earth or a hellish world marked by war, hunger, disease, and poverty? I hope that we will choose the path to a better world.

It is our destiny. It is our true purpose.

Visualizing the Ideal Society: Charting a Course

If there is no conception of an ideal society or no road map of how to get there, then we will be operating at our destination.

Its has been incredibly great to me. Despite some hardships early on in my life, I have built a number of successful businesses that have given me the economic freedom I've always desired, and that freedom means more to me than any material possession or any honors and awards I've received over the course of my career.

As we grow older, I believe we all reflect from time to time on the meaning of life and whether or not we are living a life that is filled with purpose. I've now reached a stage in my life where I have more time to think about what I can contribute based on my experiences and successes. In particular, I often think of what might constitute an ideal society.

I am a builder by nature, a toolmaker by trade. The ratio of the global auto parts powerhouse I built from scratch was ... better product for a better price. I was always driven by the challenge of making a product that was better than anything else that existed, a product that had better design, better functionality

Chapter 3

Visualizing the Ideal Society: Charting a Course

"If there is no conception of an ideal society or no road map of how to get there, then we will never arrive at our destination."

L ife has been incredibly great to me. Despite some hardships early on in my life, I have built a number of successful businesses that have given me the economic freedom I've always desired, and that freedom means more to me than any material possessions or any honors and awards I've received over the course of my career.

As we grow older, I believe we all reflect from time to time on the meaning of life and whether or not we are living a life that is filled with purpose. I've now reached a stage in my life where I have more time to think about what I can contribute based on my experiences and successes. In particular, I often think of what might constitute an ideal society.

I am a builder by nature, a toolmaker by trade. The motto of the global auto-parts powerhouse I built from scratch was *"A better product for a better price."* I was always driven by the challenge of making a product that was better than anything else that existed, a product that had better design, better functionality, better durability. I knew that if I could make a product that was not only demonstrably better but also less expensive, then I could win the business of my customer.

So at this stage in my life, I increasingly turn my attention to contemplating what it would take to build a better world. This book is my attempt to put forward a framework for what would be, in my estimation, an ideal society. Unless we first conceive what the ideal society might look like, we cannot put in place the building blocks needed to create that society. In other words, if there is no conception of an ideal society or no road map of how to get there, then we will never arrive at our destination.

In the previous chapter, I mentioned how this book is, in many ways, a search for truth and meaning. But even more than that, it is a practical exploration of what it would take to build a better world.

We cannot reasonably begin to lay the foundation of an ideal society until we first identify the key priorities for the world going forward. In essence: what must we do to not only prevent the destruction of our planet but place humanity on a path of future peace, prosperity, and harmony?

I believe one of the main priorities would be to end all wars and violent conflicts. As long as humans are killing other humans, there can be no progress. We must also enhance and extend the human charter of rights and freedoms so that more people everywhere around the world can enjoy basic human rights, such as freedom of speech and freedom of worship. Next, we need to make planet Earth sustainable by protecting the environment—the air we breathe and the water we drink. We must also establish efficient and effective governments. And we must, once and for all, eliminate poverty.

There should be no reason whatsoever that these fundamental principles, namely, no war or destruction of human life, the preservation of our environment, the enhancement of individual freedom, the establishment of good government, and the elimination of poverty, should become goals that we aggressively pursue and attain. If we adopted this mind-set and pursued these objectives, we would be able to begin an evolutionary process that would allow us to one day finally realize greater balance and harmony.

If we truly believe there should be no more wars or no more poverty or no more human suffering inflicted by our fellow humans, and if we truly believe that individual freedom is a noble goal worth pursuing, then we would begin to realize that we can only achieve these goals by seeking out common objectives and by living in complete harmony. Any other thinking will lead to the destruction of humankind.

Unfortunately, human history is filled with wars and revolutions, but until this past century, we have never had the capability of destroying our planet through catastrophic nuclear warfare. While this poses the greatest of threats, it also forces humanity to confront the reality that global warfare could bring about the destruction of all life on earth. And although we have made great progress in the past century in reducing poverty, there are still millions of people all over the world—in both impoverished, underdeveloped countries as well as in some of the richest and most advanced countries on earth—who live in dismal poverty.

I believe the centuries-old human hope of ending all wars and eliminating poverty are, for perhaps the first time in our history, within our grasp. But for that to happen, we need to continue to reduce the differences among people. When differences among people are too great, whether it be in regard to wealth or education or values, this will inevitably lead to clashes, conflict, and upheaval.

The bottom line is this: if we fail to fix the problems in our society, we face an unending future of more war and more poverty and more environmental destruction. If we continue to govern the way we currently do, we won't make any headway in regard to raising the living standards of people around the world. The political system in most democratic countries is dysfunctional, favouring the very rich and special interest groups at the expense of the majority of the country's citizens. Changing governments every few years will not solve the problem. It's our systems of government that are deeply flawed and that need to be changed.

Real leadership begins with tackling the problems confronting us and devising solutions. For example, can we fix many of the social ills that plague our societies such as homelessness and drug abuse? And can we do it by being smarter and more cost-effective instead of squandering ever greater sums of money that never seem to solve the problem? Can we devise and deliver a more practical education that is also less expensive? Can we find a way to improve our political system to make it function better? I believe the answer to all these questions is yes, and in the pages ahead, we will explore how we could go about implementing these reforms and improvements for the betterment of all.

Despite our intelligence and despite our obligation to protect and preserve the Earth, humans have caused a lot of destruction and damage to the planet and to one another through our greed and malice. And yet I strongly feel that if we change course and begin working toward the goal of creating a more perfect society, that by the year 2100, human civilization will have evolved and reached a new much higher plateau, a new era of enlightenment and prosperity for not just the few but for all.

This book serves as a guideline of sorts; it charts a path forward in the chapters that follow. But I hope that it will also serve as an inspiration, that it will motivate a whole new generation of leaders in all fields of human endeavour, whether it's the arts, politics, business, or science. Ultimately, it is my wish that this book becomes a way forward for how we could improve human existence, step by step, aspect by aspect. There is no reason why we cannot eliminate poverty, suffering, and abuse in our world or why we cannot raise educational levels, strengthen human rights, and improve living standards. We simply need to act with resolve. And we need a road map for how to get there. This book is one such road map.

Chapter 4

The Battle between Good and Evil

"The eternal conflict between good and evil is not only the central theme that runs through the teachings of the world's great religions and the classic works of literature, it's also a never-ending struggle that has guided the destiny of human civilization."

S ince the dawn of humanity, there has always been a struggle between good and evil. It's no surprise that it is one of the central themes of nearly every great book or movie ever made. And usually, it is good that triumphs in the end.

This eternal struggle captivates us. I know that I am fascinated by it. The more I reflect on it, the more questions I have: Are there real, unseen forces of good and evil at work in the universe that influence human activities? Why do some people gravitate toward evil, while others cling to goodness, even in the face of imprisonment or death—a fate that befell many people this past century who lived under the boot of various brutal dictatorships?

The ceaseless struggle between good and evil is an issue that will occupy the hearts and minds of people everywhere and in every age. And there will always be people who are guided by the pursuit of goodness and who hold to the belief that goodness can triumph over evil. This is one of the core symbolic messages of the *Pegasus and Dragon* monument that I built.

Throughout human history, we have often portrayed the forces of goodness as beautiful and friendly creatures, like angels or doves or the Pegasus, whereas the spirit of evil is usually portrayed through dangerous, fierce, and snakelike creatures like the dragon. In the colossal monument I built that will stand the test of time, the *Pegasus and Dragon* are forever entwined in this eternal struggle between good and evil that is as old as the universe itself. They have been immortalized in bronze to remind future generations of the struggle between good and evil and the need for good to prevail. To me, they are a metaphor for the human condition and a representation of the hope that good will ultimately triumph over evil.

As the owner of several major racetracks, it was always my intention to one day build a family theme park focused on horses. Gulfstream Park, located in sunny Southern Florida—America's greatest family vacation destination—was the ideal place to build that theme park. I early on decided to make the *Pegasus and Dragon* monument the centerpiece of the theme park. When we were fine-tuning the early sketches of what the monument would look like, I began doing more and more research into Greek mythology and the various legends and fables from around the world regarding dragons. And what lay at the heart of all these myths and legends was the age-old theme of good and evil. What child wouldn't be captivated by the struggle between the majestic Pegasus and the sinister dragon? Their struggle—the timeless and never-ending battle between good and evil—is a theme that visitors to the Park will enjoy for as long as the *Pegasus and Dragon* stands.

In creating the *Pegasus and Dragon* show, we want to give our guests some thrills and goose bumps. We want them to become enraptured in a world of fantasy and adventure at our park, and we want them to enjoy a classic tale of good versus evil. But we also want to provoke their minds by leaving them with a message about the fragile nature of our world, about the ways in which light and darkness, creation and destruction each have their place within the order of the universe. Most of all, we want to give our guests a hopeful message: that we can make this a better world, and that most people, if given the choice, will side with the spirit of goodness over the spirit of evil.

Domination: The Root of All Human Conflict

"One of the key challenges we face in building an ideal society is finding a way to dismantle the engines of domination—not through more endless war and revolution, but through a revolution of the mind."

The history of humankind has always been dominated by the Golden Rule: the person who has the gold makes the rules. The desire to rule over others and to dominate people is the core underlying reason for all types of human conflict.

Wars and revolutions are often fought by people who want to break free from domination. Wars are also instigated by nations who are threatened by other people who feel that these people want to repress them and dominate them.

Why is it that humans seek to dominate others? We see this domination in many forms, in many cultures, and in many ages throughout human history. It may exist in the form of a class system, where one particular class dominates the rest of society, based on their social standing or wealth. We see it in the caste system of India and in Middle Eastern theocracies.

Chapter 5

Domination: The Root of All Human Conflict

"One of the key challenges we face in building an ideal society is finding a way to dismantle the chains of domination—not through more endless war and revolution but through a revolution of the mind."

The history of humankind has always been dominated by the Golden Rule: the person who has the gold makes the rules. The desire to rule over others and to dominate people is the core underlying reason for all types of human conflict.

Wars and revolutions are often fought by people who want to break free from domination. Wars are also instigated by nations who are threatened by other people, who feel that these people want to repress them and dominate them.

Why is it that humans seek to dominate others? We see this domination in many forms, in many cultures, and in many ages throughout human history. It may exist in the form of a class system, where one particular class dominates the rest of society based on their social standing or wealth. We see it in the caste system of India and in Middle Eastern theocracies.

Regardless of race or culture, humans seem to carry within them the desire for domination—an unquenchable urge to have power over others in order to gain a particular advantage, whether it is more food or wealth or power or to gain higher standing based on knowledge or ability. And these people want to rule over others: they want to divide the world into the categories of master and servant, the hunter and the hunted. Left unchecked, the impulse to dominate can become an overwhelming and powerful force that leads to tyranny over our fellow humans.

I grew up in a time and a place that was a focal point for some the greatest conflict from the past century. I was born in Austria during the Depression. When I was still just a child, my country was taken over by Nazi Germany, one of the most brutal and ruthless regimes that ever existed, a regime responsible for the imprisonment and extermination of millions of people. Not long after annexing Austria, Nazi Germany ignited the Second World War with that country's invasion of Poland.

As a child in elementary school, I remember the Nazis introducing mandatory drills, military-style marching, and propaganda in the classroom. It was my first encounter with totalitarianism and its rigid repression and indoctrination of all individuals under its control.

I was twelve years old when the Second World War came to an end. The Nazi regime was collapsing, and our occupiers were in retreat. Our home was only a few miles away from the advancing Russian army. We could hear artillery fire and exploding bombs throughout the night for nearly a month. And when the war was finally over, it was another fanatical and dictatorial power that seized control: Communist Russia became our new rulers.

Within the span of several years, I lived under the two most oppressive political regimes of the twentieth century: Nazism and Soviet communism, two totalitarian systems that shared a compulsion to crush individual liberty and make every individual subservient to the commands of the state. Even though I was still young, I could see that these systems were incompatible with the human urge to be free.

Every totalitarian regime of the past century has had one thing in common: they were built upon the repression of individual rights and freedoms. In the end, these sorts of regimes never survive because individual domination is incompatible with the human spirit. An ideal society, therefore, must embrace and encourage the human yearning for freedom—freedom of expression and freedom to pursue your own destiny.

It is incredible at this advanced stage of civilization that human societies are still ruled by dictators and tyrants and monarchs. And even in so-called democracies, a growing segment of the population lives under the thumb of bureaucrats who serve the very rich and powerful, while the gap between the wealthy and the working class grows wider and wider.

During the past decade, we have witnessed a number of revolutions and uprisings in the Middle East as well as cries for greater freedom. It is clear to me that we in the Western world have to work harder to ensure that we spread freedom and democracy around the world. In short, we must do more to back up our belief that freedom is a basic human right that should be granted to every individual. And in order to bring about greater freedom for people everywhere, the global community should do more to spread the seeds of democracy by supporting the establishment of democratic movements and institutions.

We have too often turned a blind eye to dictatorships and corrupt political regimes that suppress the right of people to speak and worship freely. This, in turn, breeds stagnation and poverty for the majority of people living in these repressive regimes. It is hardly surprising that the countries with the least amount of freedom tend to be the countries with the lowest standards of living. Fundamentally, it boils down to this basic fact: when people have the right to speak freely and act without fear of persecution, then societies are better able to create the conditions that lead to improved living standards for their people.

Furthermore, we need to remain on guard against political or religious leaders who use religion to foster hatred or as a tool of oppression. I believe that democratic countries have a moral obligation to shine a light on religious extremists who preach hatred and seek to suppress freedom and knowledge. Despite the fact that Christians, Jews, Hindus, and Muslims all live together in harmony in many democratic countries, we unfortunately still live in a world where extremists aim to stir up hatred among people of different faiths. But in the final analysis, people of all faiths share one thing in common: the longing to be free and to seize the opportunity to build a better life for themselves and their families.

My own personal desire to be free from domination is not purely selfish. I have often said that I would never want anyone to dominate my children or my grandchildren, and if I feel that strongly, then I should never expect to be able to dominate anyone else. So one of the key challenges we face in building an ideal society is finding a way to dismantle the chains of domination—not through more endless war and revolution but through a revolution of the mind.

The clash between individualism and collectivism, symbolized by communism, fascism, and totalitarianism of all stripes, is one of the great struggles of human existence. It is, in essence, the universal human struggle to break free from the chains of domination that always seek to shackle us and mold our beliefs and our thoughts.

So the question is: can we find a way to build a world where everyone can be free? Can we find the equilibrium needed so that society can function without people dominating one another? Can we end, once and forever, the enslavement and oppression of our fellow humans?

I believe we can. Via an educational, evolutionary process, we could, over time, eliminate the aggressive instinct within humans to control and dominate other people. Our thinking process must be geared toward eliminating our destructive tendencies.

Societies that are dominated by a small group of individuals who wield power and control over everyone else never last very long. Ultimately, they fall or succumb to revolution. Nobody wants to be dominated.

Chapter 6

The Hunger for Freedom: Following Our Own Road to Happiness

"Success in life can ultimately only be measured by the degree of happiness you reach. But let me tell you, in my experience, it's a lot easier to be happy if you have some money."

Over the years, I've received a number of honorary degrees from universities recognizing my accomplishments in business. And during those occasions, I am asked to give some remarks to the graduating class of students and share some of the lessons in life I have learned over the years. I always give the students the same advice: success in life can ultimately only be measured by the degree of happiness you reach. And then I always add: But let me tell you, in my experience, it's a lot easier to be happy if you have some money.

I believe that people everywhere around the world have two basic desires: first, they crave personal freedom, which essentially means they want the right to choose their own road to happiness; and second, they want economic freedom, which essentially means they want to be financially independent. The reality is that people are not truly free unless they have economic freedom.

Within the context of a developed country, economic freedom means that most people, after having worked for twenty years, should be able to own a simple home and have enough money in the bank to live a modest lifestyle on the interest income from their savings. They would then be free from the need to work and free to nourish their hearts and minds by pursuing lifelong passions and hobbies. That, to me, is a simple snapshot of what economic freedom entails. And yet it's a shame that so few people in our society are economically free.

People hunger for freedom—the freedom to not only find individual happiness and pursue dreams and ambitions but also the freedom to be able to build a better life for themselves and their families. It is this freedom, safeguarded in our human charters of rights, that has laid the groundwork to build prosperous democratic societies in which the individual is valued more highly than the state and the rights of the individual supersede those of the government.

Fundamentally, it boils down to this irrefutable fact: when people have the right to speak freely and to speak without fear of persecution, then societies can bring about change that leads to improved living standards for their people. Without freedom of speech and expression, we can never progress and evolve to a higher level of civilization.

We in the Western world have to work much harder to ensure that we spread freedom and democracy around the world to the millions of our fellow humans who are oppressed. And we must do more to ensure that freedom is enshrined everywhere as a basic human right, a right that is bestowed on every human from birth and which is as fundamental as the right to life itself.

I worry that in many Western democracies, we have become too complacent about our freedom, which must be zealously safeguarded at all times. There is a troubling trend toward the socialization and collectivization of individuals so that people are increasingly becoming herded together in large bureaucracies and institutions where the individual gets lost. The result is that we are becoming more and more like a totalitarian society, where everyone is pressured to think and act the same and everyone increasingly looks to the state for the solution to every problem. This is how freedoms get slowly stripped away.

Freedom is one of the great longings of individuals everywhere. It is the foundation of an ideal society because without it, people would not be free to pursue their own road to happiness, to accumulate wealth, or to speak freely. There are very few ideals people in the world are willing to die for, but freedom is one of them. Freedom is nonnegotiable.

The reality is that people are not truly free unless they have economic freedom.

Chapter 7

The Pursuit of Economic Freedom

> The reality is that people are not truly free unless they have economic freedom.

Personal freedom is for me the Holy Grail, even if it means enduring every sort of hardship. But in the final analysis, personal freedom without economic freedom doesn't mean much. People are not truly free unless they have economic freedom.

What drove me as a young man was the desire to attain economic freedom. It was my key motivation in working as hard as I did to grow and build a business. There are few greater feelings of satisfaction than the feeling of knowing that you are truly free — the sort of freedom that only comes with financial independence.

Societies in the West have focused on creating great charters of human rights and freedoms, and these rights and freedoms should always be safeguarded — they have laid the groundwork for the development of prosperous democratic societies. But at the same time, we as a society must place a greater emphasis on how people can achieve economic freedom.

Chapter 7

The Pursuit of Economic Freedom

"The reality is that people are not truly free unless they have economic freedom."

Personal freedom is for me the Holy Grail, even if it means enduring every sort of hardship. But in the final analysis, personal freedom without economic freedom doesn't mean much. People are not truly free unless they have economic freedom.

What drove me as a young man was the desire to attain economic freedom. It was my key motivation in working as hard as I did to grow and build a business. There are few greater feelings of satisfaction than the feeling of knowing that you are truly free—the sort of freedom that only comes with financial independence.

Societies in the West have focused on creating great charters of human rights and freedoms, and these rights and freedoms should always be safeguarded— they have laid the groundwork for the development of prosperous democratic societies. But at the same time, we as a society must place a greater emphasis on how people can achieve economic freedom.

Since the dawn of civilization, the real crux for all sociopolitical systems has been the creation of wealth and its distribution. As a result, societies throughout the ages have developed various economic systems as a way to generate the greatest amount of wealth possible. In the past century alone, societies around the world have been governed by three main socioeconomic systems, all of which still exist in one form or another.

The three systems are Totalitarianism, Socialism/ State Enterprise, and Free Enterprise. The following is a summary of each system:

Totalitarian System or Dictatorship

Totalitarianism, which is essentially a dictatorship, is as old as human society itself. Throughout history, there have been many kinds of dictators, from kings and military generals to tyrants, such as Hitler and Stalin.

Under a Totalitarian Economic System, human rights are suppressed and economic development is often directed by military force, with the result that economic benefits are shared by relatively few people. Totalitarian systems have never been the result of humans searching for an ideal society. They are the creation of powerful and often brutal individuals who seize the levers of power to dominate and exploit their fellow citizens.

Totalitarian systems inevitably fail because they attempt to suppress the human desire for individual and economic freedom and are incompatible with the human spirit.

State Enterprise/Socialist System

One system that is the result of the human quest for an ideal society is the Socialist system, developed more than a century ago and adopted by various countries around the world, usually by way of revolution.

The Socialist system, also known as State Enterprise, is based on the philosophy that wealth should be redistributed so that there are not great differences in income levels. The State Enterprise/Socialist system is noble in theory but in practice does not work because it is not conducive to creating wealth. Individual ingenuity and incentive are stifled, and productivity deteriorates as a result. The little wealth that is produced is distributed by state bureaucrats, which eventually leads to an enormous buildup of bureaucracy. State Enterprise also results in the collectivization of individuals—also not compatible with the human spirit—and more and more people become dependent on the state for their existence. History has proven that state enterprise systems always fail, leading to greater poverty and lower living standards.

Free Enterprise System

The Free Enterprise System is extremely effective at creating wealth. It is the greatest engine of wealth creation the world has ever known. The problem with the Free Enterprise System, however, is that over time, more and more capital becomes concentrated in the hands of fewer and fewer people. This, in turn, leads to more state intervention and calls for greater redistribution of wealth. In nature, when a species does not reproduce itself, another species will take over.

Because the democratic system within a Free Enterprise society is voter-driven, this means that political parties increasingly cater to the masses by promising more and more wealth redistribution measures and socialistic programs in order to win elected office. The inevitable result is that the Free Enterprise System gets slowly pulled toward the State Enterprise/Socialist system, where the state takes and distributes a larger portion of the wealth.

So the real dilemma or crux inherent in all three major economic systems is the creation of wealth and its distribution. I strongly believe that we must do everything possible to preserve the Free Enterprise system. Without Free Enterprise, there can be no free society.

But at the same, we need to find a way within the Free Enterprise system to create a much fairer and broader-based distribution of profits—one that would give the greatest number of citizens the opportunity to achieve economic freedom. And I believe one of the best ways to do that would be to establish tax incentives for businesses to share profits with their employees. **I call this the Fair Enterprise System.**

It's unfortunate that so few businesses share profits with their employees. Sharing profits with employees is a fundamental recognition that the people who create wealth should get a fair share of that wealth.

Fair Enterprise System

The Fair Enterprise system is an alternative to the State Enterprise or Socialist system and the Free Enterprise systems. Its philosophy is based upon the principle that people desire economic freedom as well as individual freedom.

In order for Free Enterprise to avoid being absorbed by State Enterprise, businesses must create more capitalists by sharing profits and equity with workers so they can accumulate capital. However, via tax incentives, businesses can be encouraged to give a greater number of workers the right to participate in capital building.

Ultimately, our human charters of rights need to be augmented and fortified with economic charters of rights, including the right of workers to accumulate wealth through equity and profit participation. Economic charters of rights will lead to economic democracies, and economic democracies are the basis for democracy itself.

Economic Systems

Fair enterprise is designed to prevent the free enterprise system from being pulled toward the state enterprise system

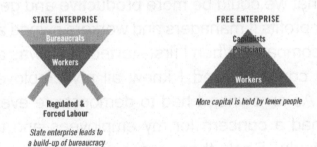

State enterprise leads to a build-up of bureaucracy

More capital is held by fewer people

FAIR ENTERPRISE

Workers Become Capitalists

Economic Charters of Rights give workers the right to participate in capital building and result in enhanced wealth creation and its fair distribution

Chapter 8

Creating an Ownership Society

"It's amazing what ownership does to people. When people own things, their whole mentality changes."

The automotive-parts powerhouse I built from a one-man tool ship enjoyed great success over the years. Many people have asked me: what was the secret to our success? And I have always responded that if you wanted to know what made Magna make tick—what drove the company to be the very best and what drove our people to work better, harder, smarter—then you needed to understand what my Fair Enterprise philosophy was all about.

The development of Fair Enterprise sprang from my belief that we could be more productive and generate greater profits if managers and workers owned a piece of the company. When I first started out, I was a small private company, and I knew all my employees by name. As an owner, I had to demonstrate every day that I had a concern for my employees and treated them fairly. Back then, we shared profits on an informal basis. But as we grew larger, I wanted to have an environment where managers and workers got a portion of the profits and became part owners.

When my company merged with a publicly traded company, I was able to give employees not only a piece of the profits but shares in the corporation as well, making them part owners. There's nothing like ownership to instil pride and create drive and hustle. I felt strongly that if employees knew they had a real and tangible stake in the company's success, they would be more motivated to produce a better product for a better price. That, in essence, is what Fair Enterprise is all about.

But I have always wondered: what would happen if we could do the very same not just within a company but within an entire country? What if we were able to introduce those Fair Enterprise ownership and profit-participation principles on a national level? In other words: what if we could transform our society into a society of owners?

It's amazing what ownership does to people. When people own things, their whole mentality changes. They become more careful, more concerned, more committed. They have a whole new outlook.

Think about it this way: when you rent a hotel room, you're not as concerned if you leave the lights on when you go out or you let the water run. Similarly, if you rent a house or an apartment, it's never the same as if you own your own shelter. When you invest your own money into buying a house or condominium, no matter how small or modest, you will take greater care of it.

I believe an ideal society must look at ways to enhance ownership and create an ownership mentality. For example, if we provided tax incentives to companies that offered employees equity and profit participation, this would give a much greater number of workers the chance to become part owners. This in turn would help unleash greater economic productivity since ownership would give employees a stronger stake in the outcome of the business they work for.

There would be a strengthened commitment to excellence, efficiency, and innovation that comes about when people have a stake in the outcome—when they own a piece of the machinery they're working on and get a slice of the profits they produce. Creating a society of owners is a surefire way to build a stronger, prouder, and more productive society.

The following is an example of the profit-sharing principles contained in Magna's Corporate Constitution:

MAGNA'S CORPORATE CONSTITUTION

Employee Equity and Profit Participation
Ten percent of Magna's qualifying profit before tax will be allocated to eligible employees. These funds will be used for the purchase of Magna shares in trust for eligible employees and for cash distributions to eligible employees, recognizing length of service.

Shareholder Profit Participation
Magna will distribute, on average over a three-year period, not less than 20 percent of its annual net profit after tax to shareholders.

Management Profit Participation
To obtain long-term contractual commitment, Magna provides a compensation arrangement to corporate management which allows for base salaries comparable to industry standards, plus incentive bonuses, in total, of up to 6 percent of its profit before tax.

Research and Development
Magna will allocate a minimum of 7 percent of its profit before tax for research and development to ensure its long-term viability.

Social Responsibility
Magna will allocate a maximum of 2 percent of its profit before tax for charitable, cultural, educational and political purposes to support the basic fabric of society.

Magna's Profit-Sharing Formula

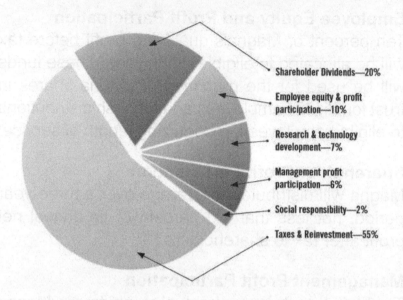

Shareholder Dividends—20%

Employee equity & profit participation—10%

Research & technology development—7%

Management profit participation—6%

Social responsibility—2%

Taxes & Reinvestment—55%

At the heart of Magna's Corporate Constitution is a profit-sharing formula that predetermines how the company's annual profits are divided among its key stakeholders: employees, investors, management, and society.

Chapter 9

Imagination: The Wellspring of New Knowledge and Creativity

"With imagination, the possibilities for human development are endless."

O f all the human skills and attributes, none is greater, in my view, than imagination. Imagination is the wellspring of all knowledge.

Pure knowledge has limitations. We cannot know everything, and even when we do gain new knowledge, there is only so much that we can do with it. Imagination, on the other hand, has no limitations—it is sheer blue sky, not bound by the past or by conventional notions of how things should be. Rather, imagination is guided by an idea of how things could be.

The desire to think about what could be—rather than what merely is—is also a powerful human urge. Some might argue that it is as powerful a need as the need to breathe and eat. And unlike freedom or thought or speech, imagination can never be stifled or constrained.

Our greatest inventions, sociopolitical and economic systems, and works of art, all originated in our imagination and then were refined over time using the tools of human knowledge and skill. In short, everything that is dramatically new or different since the beginning of time has been the product of human imagination, and all the great and lasting human advances were accomplished by people of imagination.

I find it incomprehensible, therefore, that we do not put more emphasis on encouraging imagination. The human mind has an incredible capacity for ingenuity and creativity—the by-products of imagination—and I'm a firm believer that we all possess enormous untapped potential that can be tapped by using our imagination. The process for fostering imaginative thinking should begin when our children are very young and should be a key focus throughout their schooling since it is a skill as important as scientific analysis or critical thinking. Either way, we must make a greater effort to inspire and promote individual ingenuity and creativity.

There is no future without imagination because in the absence of imagination and innovation, there is only a continuation of the present. Perhaps the greatest outpouring of human imagination occurred last century, when new technologies such as trains, cars, and planes reshaped the way we lived, accelerating the pace of human life and enhancing individual freedom by providing greater mobility. For millennia, we dreamed of one day being able to fly through the skies above us and we dreamed of one day travelling into outer space and landing on the moon. Our imagination was the spark that enabled us to achieve those dreams.

In the chapters ahead, we will look at ways in which we can envision the society of the future. In short, we will be engaged in the process of rethinking the world of tomorrow—abandoning some of the older and unworkable features of a bygone era and thinking about what new features will be needed by people in the century that lies ahead.

Invention and innovation are the twin children of imagination, the tools that help us move society forward and improve the quality of life for people everywhere. Ultimately, we need to harness the power of imagination in order to expand knowledge and enhance the quality of life experienced by all the inhabitants of our planet.

Without imagination, we will become a decaying society. With imagination, the possibilities for human development are endless.

Chapter 10

The Quest for the Natural

"In a world that is increasingly mechanical, artificial, and man-made, humans long for that which is natural."

Nature gives us a good guideline—a pattern or template we could follow—of what would constitute an ideal society. The truth is, we need to be in unison with the natural order of the universe if we are going to be successful at constructing the ideal society. We cannot fight against nature; we must live within the framework laid down by nature's invisible and unbreakable laws.

We know, for example, that nature favors harmony and balance, and we also know that the greatest human civilizations in history have always placed a high value on these two qualities.

In a world that is increasingly mechanical, artificial, and man-made, humans long for that which is natural. We want to ensure the preservation of our natural environment, our lakes and rivers and forests, and we increasingly desire natural foods and natural materials.

We are also undeniably subject to the natural environment—everything from the air we inhale to the water we drink and the food we eat. But we've strayed too far from what is natural and moved too much toward what is artificial and man-made. We've now reached a point where we need to reverse that.

Although we should never stop seeking to develop new and better technologies and scientific advances, we must also remember that we will never be smarter than Mother Nature. The natural laws of the universe will always reign supreme.

I believe we need to revert to a more natural way of living, one in which we live and work together in harmony with nature. When I built my first horse farm in Kentucky in the late 1980s, I discovered a number of Native American artifacts on my property, including arrowheads. The artifacts belonged to a group of tribes of pre-Columbian Native Americans known as the Adena. Their culture prized agriculture and trade and regarded nature with reverence and respect—a reverence and respect that we would do well to adopt.

Today, I pay tribute to the Adena through the names of my horse racing stable, Adena Springs, and my all-natural, grass-fed cattle ranch, Adena Farms, as well as Adena Meadows, a housing development, Adena Golf and Country Club, and Adena Grill, a restaurant located near the *Pegasus and Dragon* monument in Hallandale Beach, Florida. The Adena logo for all these companies prominently feature an arrow and arrowhead in the capital letter *A* representing the name Adena.

For me, nothing symbolizes the power and beauty of nature more than the horse. Early in my career, I was heavily involved in building my automotive-parts business. Magna, the company I founded, was growing rapidly and producing hundreds and hundreds of different automotive components, everything from gears and brackets to latches. I was working fourteen to sixteen hours a day, including weekends, for many years. I desperately needed a diversion or outlet—something completely outside the mechanized and industrialized world of automotive manufacturing, something that would provide an organic counterbalance to the metallic world I was immersed in. And for me, that counterbalance was horses.

I saw an ad in the newspaper from a farmer who was selling a riding horse. I had just moved to a 150-acre farm out in the country and thought it would be enjoyable to have a horse that I could ride through the fields and rolling hills on my property like John Wayne in some old Western movie.

The farmer who sold me my first horse ended up taking me to the racetrack one day, where I developed an ever greater passion and fascination for horses. That fascination eventually turned into a labor of love:

I became a horse owner and breeder and, over a period of several decades, built one of the world's most successful thoroughbred racing stables. Horses have remained for me that vital connection to nature.

Horses represent a powerful bond with the natural world that we have lost in developed countries during the past century because of urbanization and technological advancement. Around the turn of the last century, as the automobile began to gain popularity, there were fewer and fewer horses being bred. But prior to that, every farm in America had a few horses. People not only owned horses but loved them—there was a much greater connection between horses and people a century ago.

From the mid-1940s to the early 1960s—the heyday of thoroughbred racing in America—many farmers still had horses, but they were slowly beginning to disappear. Their gradual decline in numbers led to a weakening of the binding ties that people once had with horses. Perhaps not surprisingly, attendance at thoroughbred racetracks also started to deteriorate.

The dissolving bond between humans and horses is to me a symptom of our growing detachment from nature itself, which in turn leads to the mistaken notion that we somehow exist apart from nature. And this attitude leads to many of the activities we increasingly engage in, such as dumping poisons and toxins into our rivers and oceans or spraying crops and vegetation with pesticides and herbicides.

But there is a growing awareness that we can no longer destroy the natural environment without dire consequences to ourselves and all other life on Earth. It is one reason, for example, why more and more people are turning away from foods laced with chemicals, hormones, antibiotics, and genetically modified organisms and moving instead toward all-natural, organic foods.

I became a part of the movement toward all-natural foods when I established my ranch in Ocala, Florida—ninety-five thousand acres of rolling pastures, fields, and forests where cattle, chicken, and pigs roam and graze freely. The foremost principle at our farm is that we do everything we can to avoid pain and stress to our animals. We employ the highest standards of animal welfare, and all the animals at our farm are raised in a completely natural environment throughout their entire lives. We feed our animals only natural foods—no added growth hormones, no antibiotics, no GMOs, and no animal by-products. We're an eco-friendly farm that uses sustainable, free-range farming methods. Most of the time, we herd our cattle with cowboys on horseback and herding dogs—exactly the way we used to raise cattle more than a century ago.

More and more, people want to restore our links with nature and to live more fully in harmony with our natural surroundings. Doing so is an important step to building a better world. The quest for an ideal society begins with the quest to live more in tune with the natural world we live in.

Chapter 11

America: A Role Model for the World

"Free enterprise made America great and prosperous, and free enterprise is one of the pillars of a free society."

When it comes to countries that the world should look to in terms of the foundation of an ideal society, one stands head and shoulders above the rest: the United States of America.

Whether it's democratic rights and freedoms or living standards and innovation, America is a shining example as a role model for the world despite the problems it continues to wrestle with, including a sizeable percentage of its population living in poverty.

Naturally, some may point to other countries as superior role models, but in my view, as someone who was born in Europe and who has done business on virtually every continent in the world, I can confidently say that none comes close to the USA.

I was born and raised in Austria. I worked for a period in Switzerland. And in the last thirty years, I have spent half my time in Europe where I helped turn the company I founded into a global corporation. From my own personal and business experience during that time, I can say that Europe is developing more and more into a "politicratic" society—a phrase I created to describe the toxic mixture of political influence seeping into every aspect of an overly bureaucratic society. The end result is a growing number of complicated rules governing all aspects of life—everything from taxation and labor to education—all leading to a massive buildup of bureaucracy, which in turn results in the arteries of commerce becoming calcified and blocked. I see no hope for Europe. It is slowly suffocating.

In terms of a historical perspective, China has always been very advanced but was burdened for many generations with bad leadership. It appears the country is now making enormous progress in terms of economic development and enhanced living standards for its people. Of course, in a dictatorship, it is much easier to plan and build entire cities, roads, and airports. However, the key question with China is: will the country advance toward a true democracy based on human rights? Like many others, I truly hope it will.

Russia is very much like China, a rising superpower with military might that rivals the USA and an economy blessed with an abundance of natural resources as well as advanced high-tech industries. Since the overthrow of the Communist Soviet empire under the leadership of Mikhail Gorbachev, one of the greatest leaders of the twentieth century, Russia appears to have slid back in terms of its progress toward becoming a true democracy. But like China, many continue to hold out hope that Russia will also continue along the path to a more democratic society with strong human rights and greater freedom.

In South America, the discrepancy between the rich and the poor has always been great, and there has been very little progress made in terms of wider wealth distribution. The countries of South America, particularly Brazil, need to exert greater effort when it comes to raising the living standards of their poorest citizens. And many of the countries on that continent are crippled by corruption and elitism.

Africa, on the other hand, is still suffering the effects of being ruled for several centuries by colonial powers. Would the countries of Africa be better off today had they not been subject to colonial rule? One could argue that they likely would be. Even if this was so, there is no going back for the countries of Africa. It will be a long time before they find their way in the new global economy, but some of them may yet emerge as economic powerhouses, given their rich resources.

Incredibly, there are still numerous countries throughout the world ruled by dictators and religious tyrants or dynasties. Many of the countries throughout the Middle East fall into one of these categories. So it is highly unlikely that people around the world would turn to one of these countries, with poor track records in regard to human rights and freedoms, as a model that the world should strive to emulate.

Which brings us back to America. I believe the USA is still the greatest country in the world. It is a relatively young country when compared to most others in the world. It is full of hope and optimism and is made up of people who are the descendants of pioneers and hardy immigrants—people with the guts and courage to leave their homeland and start a new life in a new world.

America should never take democracy for granted and must always stand on guard to preserve freedom at home and abroad. As the undisputed leader of the free world, it is vital that America continues to be at the forefront of advanced weapons technology in order to protect the country and its allies. In order to ensure that America remains the global leader in weapons systems, it should divert a large portion of the money it currently spends on overseas military bases and put that money instead into developing the world's most sophisticated and advanced weapons technology as a deterrent to other countries that might harbor a hostile intent. But at the same time, America should never fire the first shot in any conflict.

The USA has some social and economic cancers that need to be cut out—everything from racism and crime to poverty. It needs to come to grips with the fact it is not winning the war on poverty, especially in some of the inner cities which are decaying at an alarming rate.

Despite these issues, it is legitimate to ask if America can still be held up as a role model for the world. However, among all the countries on earth, I believe that none comes close to the United States of America in terms of being the starting point for the ideal society.

Although I wasn't born in the USA, I've spent decades living and working there. I value the principles of freedom that America stands for, and I admire the entrepreneurial can-do spirit of Americans. I believe that America is one of the few remaining countries in the world where free enterprise still has a chance to survive. Free enterprise made America great and prosperous, and free enterprise is one of the pillars of a free society.

We have now spelled out some of the foundational elements of an ideal society. These include the pursuit of goodness, the promotion and preservation of freedom, and the protection and cultivation of nature. In the chapters ahead, we will look at some of the building blocks of the ideal society—everything from the economy and the government to education and health care.

The Promises of an Ideal Society

Ultimately, an ideal society can only be measured by the way it looks after people who cannot look after themselves.

In shaping the framework of an ideal society, we first need to identify what its priorities are. We also need to agree on the minimum standards of a civilized society.

Democratic societies have great human rights that include freedom of religion and freedom of speech, among many others. But none of these charters of rights have provisions dealing with the fundamental needs of human existence: food and medicine and shelter, without which we could not survive.

I believe we therefore need to embed within our human charters of rights the following core principles:

- the right to food, in order to never be hungry;
- the right to shelter, in order to never be homeless or exposed to the elements; and
- the right to health care, in order to never die or become sick from an illness that could have been treated.

Chapter 12

The Priorities of an Ideal Society

"Ultimately, an ideal society can only be measured by the way it looks after people who cannot look after themselves."

In shaping the framework of an ideal society, we first need to identify what its priorities are. We also need to agree on the minimum standards of a civilized society.

Democratic societies have great human rights that include freedom of religion and freedom of speech, among many others. But none of these charters of rights have provisions dealing with the fundamental needs of human existence: food and medicine and shelter, without which we could not survive.

I believe we therefore need to embed within our human charters of rights the following core principles:

- the right to food, in order to never be hungry;
- the right to shelter, in order to never be homeless or exposed to the elements; and
- the right to health care, in order to never die or become sick from an illness that could have been treated.

These, for me, are bedrock principles that are nonnegotiable and that any civilized society would endorse.

But there are also other fundamental rights to uphold and protect: the right to drink water, for example, and the right to breathe air. These are necessities for life itself. And when these rights are combined with the rights guaranteeing freedom from hunger and access to shelter and medical care, then you begin to have the framework of what would constitute the minimum standards in an ideal society. Ultimately, an ideal society can only be measured by the way it looks after people who cannot look after themselves.

But once we enshrine these fundamental rights, we then need to begin mapping out the priorities of the ideal society—the issues and areas that must be addressed if we are to move society toward a higher, more advanced, and more civilized plateau.

One of the key themes that runs through this book is the need to strengthen democratic rights and freedoms and to give a greater number of people the right to pursue their own road to happiness. But in order for us to achieve these noble and worthwhile goals, we must also ensure that the world in which we live is economically strong, free, and healthy. And for that to happen, our world must be sustainable in regard to the number of people the Earth can house and feed, and it must be sustainable in terms of eliminating the environmental damage we continue to inflict upon the water, air, and soil. We need to instill in everyone the view that we should never be a burden on the state unless we experience the misfortune of falling ill or becoming unable to care for ourselves.

As someone who has worked in business for more than sixty years, who has built factories in over thirty countries around the globe, who has met with high-ranking CEOs and world leaders, and who accumulated a wealth of knowledge and experiences across a wide spectrum of society, I believe I can contribute some valuable insights into the functioning of government and the key pillars of society.

In identifying the priorities for establishing an ideal society, the first is clearly the economy. Specifically, we need to realize that we must first create wealth before we can distribute it. In an earlier chapter, I highlighted the fact that Free Enterprise has a flaw—namely, that capital is held by fewer and fewer people and there are fewer and fewer capitalists. The laws of nature tell us that when a species begins to decline, another species will take over.

Our number 1 priority, therefore, should be to find ways in which we can turn workers into capitalists. In essence, every worker should have the opportunity to become a capitalist through the accumulation of wealth. And one of the best ways for that to happen would be to give workers the opportunity to share in a portion of the profits they help make. In other words, it would be a fundamental recognition that the economy is driven by three forces: smart managers, investors, and hardworking employees, and all three have a moral right to the outcome, which is profits.

I have come to the conclusion that the United States is the only country left in the world where the Free Enterprise system may have a chance to survive. Europe, the region of the world where I was born and raised, has become completely socialistic. History has shown us time and again that when countries adopt socialistic policies, which are essentially built upon the redistribution of wealth, then those countries eventually become poorer and poorer.

Other priorities include the reform for our education system, which is the foundation for developing productive, intelligent, and skilled citizens, as well as the reform of our system of government, which sets the course for a society through the policies and programs it implements.

Depoliticizing government, simplifying the tax system, reducing government spending and debt, reforming our education and health-care systems—these are just some of the issues we need to address if we are to build an ideal society. These various systems, whether they reside primarily within the government or the economy or society at large, are all interconnected and interrelated.

In the chapters that follow, we will take an in-depth and detailed look at creating the building blocks of a better society—a society with greater harmony and equilibrium, a society that gives a greater number of people the chance to live a better life.

Chapter 10

Restoring Balance to the Economy

"One of the chief problems over the past several decades is that we've focused too much on the redistribution of wealth rather than on the creation of wealth."

W e need to remember that if the economy doesn't function, nothing else will. Our health care, our education, our arts and entertainment, our social welfare systems—they all feed off the wealth that business creates.

But we are no longer creating wealth in the West at the same rate as in the past century. Our economies are no longer functioning the way they should.

There are two major trends that have derailed our economic progress in the West over the past five decades. The first is the slow and steady slide from a predominantly Free Enterprise system toward a State Enterprise or socialistic system, and the second is the detrimental shift from a real economy based on manufacturing products to a financial economy built on financial transactions.

In the past several decades, we've witnessed a growing trend throughout the West toward the adoption of socialistic policies—policies that are focused on the

Chapter 13

Restoring Balance to the Economy

"One of the chief problems over the past several decades is that we've focused too much on the redistribution of wealth rather than on the creation of wealth."

We need to remember that if the economy doesn't function, nothing else will. Our health care, our education, our arts and entertainment, our social welfare systems—they all feed off the wealth that business creates.

But we are no longer creating wealth in the West at the same rate as in the past century. Our economies are no longer functioning the way they should.

There are two major trends that have derailed our economic progress in the West over the past five decades: the first is the slow and steady slide from a predominantly Free Enterprise system toward a State Enterprise or socialistic system and the second is the detrimental shift from a real economy based on manufacturing products to a financial economy built on financial transactions.

In the past several decades, we've witnessed a growing trend throughout the West toward the adoption of socialistic policies—policies that are focused on the *distribution* of wealth rather than on the *creation* of wealth. Even though I come from a working class family, I long ago came to the conclusion that the socialistic philosophy, based on wealth distribution, will not help raise the living standards of people.

Europe has travelled fairly far down the road toward socialism, and the same sorts of policies that have become entrenched there are gaining ground in the USA. As a result, I believe we've reached a dangerous tipping point where more and more people are taking out of our economy and fewer and fewer people are contributing to it, and a growing number of citizens are becoming dependent on the state for their subsistence.

When I was chairman of Magna International Inc., our company became the first manufacturer in North America to open a factory in the former Soviet Union following the fall of the Berlin Wall. We built a factory in the Ukraine and then, several years later, in what was once the Soviet Republic of East Germany.

The two former nations of West Germany and East Germany, now united once again, provided a striking illustration of the differences between Free Enterprise and State Enterprise. A divided nation of people lived under the two different economic systems for nearly half a century. West Germany, operating within a Free Enterprise system, became one of the world's most productive and successful economies. In contrast,

East Germany, after operating for many years under a socialist system, experienced a drastic increase in poverty and was not able to feed its people. Its infrastructure crumbled, causing significant damage to the environment, and its economy ultimately broke down. East Germany was an example of the economic reality that we must first create wealth before we can distribute it.

Over the last few years, I've become especially alarmed at the rapid deterioration of the manufacturing base in most developed countries. Walk down the aisles of any major department store and you will see a stark reminder that fewer and fewer products are made in the West. Wherever I go in North America and Western Europe, I see more and more warehouses and fewer and fewer factories. You don't have to be a great economist to know why: we are manufacturing and exporting fewer products and instead importing a greater number of goods produced elsewhere— everything from toys and TVs to cell phones and computers. Even the fruits and vegetables we eat are increasingly grown in other countries and shipped in.

Since the financial meltdown of 2008 that caused widespread economic damage around the world, there has been little or no discussion of what steps we should take to prevent a similar financial earthquake from occurring again. We have not changed any of the underlying conditions that caused the collapse nor have we put a leash on the wildly unregulated financial systems that created the meltdown.

What's worse, we've tried to correct the problem by pumping trillions of dollars into the economy to stave off a full-scale collapse. All this has been done with borrowed money, and governments around the world have shown little or no inclination to curtail their spending.

This borrowing and subsequent buildup of debt is masking the real economic decline that is taking place. In the West, our fridges are still filled with food, but our living standards are eroding. There is a slow but sure shift of economic wealth and power taking place, and it is moving from the West to the East.

Businesses and countries have to continually adjust to shifting economic conditions, whether they are changes brought about by technological innovation or changes unleashed by forces such as globalization or deregulation. When these sort of massive changes ripple through the economy, like the shock waves of an earthquake, they trigger unforeseen changes in other industries as well and can even alter society. And all these changes ultimately have an impact on jobs and wages. Evolution and change in business are inevitable and relentless. In the end, all businesses are faced with two choices: either continuously change or get left behind.

I have been concerned for a long time now that we as a society are moving away from making things. **We have drifted away from a real economy, where we manufacture products, to a predominantly financial economy**—in other words, an economy where you have more and more people shuffling papers. But you can't build houses or machines with paper and you can't eat paper.

We have become less and less preoccupied with creating real wealth and more and more engaged in the process of transferring and redistributing the declining wealth that we do generate. At the end of the day, the deterioration of our manufacturing sector has a great impact on the overall economy, and it robs us of one of our chief engines of technological innovation.

We need to be careful that we don't dismantle our farms and factories and end up importing everything from abroad. If we continue to go down that road, we will lose a lot of good-paying jobs—jobs that will never return. We will also lose some of our economic independence. And most importantly, we will watch our exports decline and, with it, our high standard of living.

In order to create new jobs—as well as keep the jobs we currently have—our number 1 priority should be to stimulate greater manufacturing and production in order to reduce imports and create more balanced trade. Companies that manufacture products create more and better-paying jobs than companies that merely import goods. We need to turn our warehouses into factories.

The implications of the erosion of the real economy are significant: a decline in manufacturing capability will lead to a decline in a country's technology base and technical know-how. A strong and vibrant manufacturing sector, with the technology base it rests on, is vital to our long-term strategic interests. The manufacturing industry and its supply base jointly develop a vast array of technologies and products—everything from sophisticated electronics to new composite metals and plastics. These technologies have applications not only in a wide range of industries but also in the defense industry, which is vital for safeguarding democracies around the world and our rights and freedoms here at home.

This shift away from a real economy to a financial economy has not only resulted in the loss of good-paying jobs in the manufacturing sector, but it was also a major contributing factor in the economic meltdown of 2008, when governments throughout the West had to pay trillions of dollars to bail out financial institutions, leaving a legacy of worthless financial assets, deficits, and debt. In most countries, taxpayers ended up shouldering the enormous cost of the bailouts and will continue paying for those bailouts for many years to come.

We need to reverse the trend toward a financial economy and return to a real economy focused on developing and manufacturing products that creates employment.

One of the chief problems over the past several decades is that we've focused too much on the redistribution of wealth rather than on the creation of wealth. We need to rebalance that by focusing more intensely on wealth creation. In a free society, the best way to create wealth is by being more productive, and **the best way for a society to be more productive is for workers to receive a fair share of the wealth they help to create**. Sharing profits with employees is a proven formula for growth because when workers have a tangible stake in the company's financial success, they are more motivated to produce a better product for a better price. Incentivizing companies to adopt employee profit sharing ensures that wealth is distributed more evenly and fairly throughout the economy rather than remaining concentrated in the hands of relatively few individuals.

The economy is driven by three forces: smart management, hardworking employees, and investors. All three of these stakeholders have a moral right to share in the financial outcome of the business.

Profit sharing would generate more income for employees and more money would be spent on consumer products. This would fuel economic growth and generate higher tax revenue for governments. Sharing profits would also make businesses more competitive because when workers have a tangible stake in the company's financial success, they are more productive. Most importantly, the implementation of profit-sharing policies would lead to a much fairer and wider distribution of capital and would help to narrow the growing gap in our society between the wealthy and the workers.

I believe that every man and woman wakes up each morning with the desire to build a better life for themselves and their families. We need to create an environment that will give a greater number of citizens the opportunity to accumulate wealth and attain economic freedom.

By implementing some simple but powerful common-sense changes, I believe we can reverse the trend toward economic stagnation and decline and make our economies strong once again. A strong economy would also give governments a greater ability to invest in education, health, and infrastructure while providing assistance to those individuals who cannot provide for themselves. Most of the reforms and proposals contained within this chapter are simple, straightforward policies that can be easily implemented. If adopted, we would generate increased economic growth, successfully raise our living standards, place our economy back on the path of prosperity, and build the framework for a more prosperous future.

Sheathed in dazzling bronze, the iconic Pegasus and Dragon monument pays homage to the courage, speed, and power of the horse and is a classic symbol of the struggle between good and evil.

The world's largest horse sculpture, Pegasus and Dragon stands ten stories tall and weighs 715 tons.

An aerial overview showing the Pegasus and Dragon monument next to Gulfstream Park in Hallandale Beach, Florida.

Assembling the sculpture: Pegasus and Dragon was built by more than 500 workers and 70 sculptors, then shipped to Gulfstream Park in Florida in freight containers holding 4,750 pieces of steel and 1,250 bronze sections.

The spectacular fountain show at the Pegasus and Dragon monument.

The Pegasus statue towers over a domed structure that will house a cinema where visitors will be able to experience a dramatization of the battle between Pegasus and Dragon that raises some of the timeless themes and issues explored in this book.

Chapter 14

Making Taxation Fairer and Simpler

"The tax system in most Western countries is broken and unbalanced, crushing individuals and businesses with higher and higher rates of taxation, favoring importers over exporters and financial firms over manufacturers."

When it comes to the health of our economy, the measure that has the single greatest bearing is the tax system. More than any other economic lever, the tax system determines whether the economy grows, shrinks, or stagnates.

But it seems more and more that the only segment of the economy that benefits from the tax system is the growing multitude of tax lawyers and tax specialists who make a living deciphering our incredibly complex tax laws for their clients. And usually, these experts are the very same people who had a hand in writing the tax laws to begin with—a massive conflict of interest. This conflict of interest is enriching a growing class of tax consultants while choking the productive juices of our economy.

The tax system in most Western countries is broken and unbalanced, crushing individuals and businesses with higher and higher rates of taxation, favoring importers over exporters and financial firms over manufacturers. It is overly complicated and riddled with loopholes, while providing tax breaks and privileges to special interests, including the wealthy and the financial institutions that feed off the system. Restoring balance means injecting fairness, simplicity, and transparency into our tax system.

The Taxpayer Advocate Service (TAS) is an independent organization within the Internal Revenue Service (IRS) that was established in the mid-1990s. Its mandate is to protect taxpayers by identifying the most serious tax problems facing the nation, outlined each year in an Annual Report to Congress, which proposes legislative changes to fix the problems. For years now, the TAS reports have repeatedly identified "the complexity of the tax code as the single most serious problem facing taxpayers" and have urged Congress to take action. But nothing ever happens? Why?

The TAS has stated that the tax code is riddled with problems that sap economic productivity and efficiency, including requiring taxpayers to devote excessive time to file their tax return; requiring a majority of taxpayers to shoulder additional costs related to tax compliance (e.g., hiring tax lawyers and tax preparers, purchasing tax preparation software, etc.); and by undermining trust in the tax system. In fact, the TAS has conducted a national survey of taxpayers and found that only 16 percent believe the tax laws are fair. The TAS found this "extraordinary lack of public trust in the method by which our government is funded profoundly disturbing." But is it any wonder that taxpayers do not believe the tax laws are fair?

What's even more baffling is that the IRS itself has stated that the US tax code is "so complex the IRS has difficulty administering it." The fact is, the current system is archaic, hard to understand, and increasingly cumbersome to administer. On top of this, the unmanageable nature of the tax system has spawned a whole new professional class of tax lawyers and tax professionals who interpret and decode the thousands of pages of swampy language that comprise our tax code. It is astounding that there has not been a greater nationwide uproar and insurrection over our tax system. After all, it was the issue of unfair and arbitrary taxation that sparked the American Revolution.

Over the years, when I spoke at Chamber of Commerce dinners or business school lectures, I often used to say that we need to create a tax system that a high school student could understand—something simple, straightforward, and clear-cut, with no loopholes. It was a common-sense statement that always sparked loud applause from the audience.

We need a tax system that is totally transparent, simple to administer, easy to understand, and with no loopholes and a tax return that is no longer than a single sheet of paper. If we developed such a system, we could dramatically reduce government overhead and free businesses from the time spent complying with tax filings and preparing for tax audits—time that ultimately increases the final cost of the product or service provided by the business.

The tax codes have become more and more complicated and cumbersome with each passing year, requiring a growing army of lawyers and tax specialists and financial experts to navigate their way through a maze of rules and regulations.

The following is just one of many impossible-to-decipher examples of complexity from the US tax code. Section 467(e)(1) reads:

> **The term "constant rental amount" means, with respect to any section 467 rental agreement, the amount which, if paid as of the close of each lease period under the agreement, would result in an aggregate present value equal to the present value of the aggregate payments required under the agreement.**

And below is another from Section 341:

> **For purposes of subsection (a)(1), a corporation shall not be considered**

to be a collapsible corporation with respect to any sale or exchange of stock of the corporation by a shareholder, if, at the time of such sale or exchange, the sum of - (A) the net unrealized appreciation in subsection (e) assets of the corporation (as defined in paragraph (5)(A)), plus (B) if the shareholder owns more than 5 percent in value of the outstanding stock of the corporation the net unrealized appreciation in assets of the corporation (other than assets described in subparagraph (A)) which would be subsection (e) assets under clauses (i) and (iii) of paragraph (5)(A) if the shareholder owned more than 20 percent in value of such stock, plus (C) if the shareholder owns more than 20 percent in value of the outstanding stock of the corporation and owns, or at any time during the preceding 3-year period owned, more than 20 percent in value of the outstanding stock of any other corporation more than 70 percent in value of the assets of which are, or were at any time during which such shareholder owned during such 3-year period more than 20 percent in value of the outstanding stock, assets similar or related in service or use to assets comprising more than 70 percent in value of the assets of the corporation, the net unrealized appreciation in assets of the corporation (other than assets described in subparagraph (A)) which would be subsection (e) assets under clauses (i) and (iii) of paragraph (5)(A) if the determination whether the property, in the hands of such shareholder, would be property gain from the sale or exchange of which would under any provision of this chapter be considered in whole or in part as ordinary income, were made - (i) by treating any sale or exchange by such shareholder of stock in such other corporation within the preceding 3-year period (but only if at the time of such sale or exchange the shareholder owned more than 20 percent in value of the outstanding stock in such other corporation) as a sale or exchange by such shareholder of his proportionate share of the assets of such other corporation, and (ii) by treating any liquidating sale or exchange of property by such other corporation within such 3-year period (but only if at the time of such sale or exchange

the shareholder owned more than 20 percent in value of the outstanding stock in such other corporation) as a sale or exchange by such shareholder of his proportionate share of the property sold or exchanged, does not exceed an amount equal to 15 percent of the net worth of the corporation.

There is simply no way any person can figure out the tax laws governing business. I can't count the number of times during the course of my career when we were faced with a business tax matter that needed a clear-cut answer. After countless meetings and thousands of dollars in fees, no one could put forward a definitive answer. The plain fact is, the tax system is overly complicated, too vague, and too difficult to understand. The arteries of commerce are becoming clogged as a result.

The tax system has become a drag on economic growth and a drain on national expenditures, requiring a huge bureaucracy to administer and oversee the tangle of tax legislation. Each year, another several layers get added. These new laws never make it easier to produce goods and services but almost always end up adding additional costs that are borne by consumers and businesses.

The implementation of a fairer and simpler tax system would be relatively easy and could be done without disrupting the collection of taxes.

A revamped tax system should recognize that a successful business requires three forces to create wealth: good management, hardworking employees, and investors. All three of these stakeholders have a moral right to share in the financial outcome. Magna, the company I founded, has shown for the past half-century that sharing profits with employees is a proven and powerful formula for growth. When workers have a tangible stake in the company's financial success, they are more motivated to produce a better product for a better price.

To streamline our tax system and unshackle small businesses from the red tape and regulations associated with tax filing while at the same time boosting productivity by allowing employees to participate in wealth creation, I would propose a simplified sales tax.

Here's how it would work:

Small businesses (any company with up to a hundred employees) would have the choice of either paying the existing tax rate or a simplified tax rate based on annual sales. Companies that choose to pay the simplified tax rate would only pay 2 percent of their total sales in taxes, and they would pay an additional 2 percent of their annual sales to employees in the form of profit sharing—half in cash payments and half invested in a guaranteed employee pension fund. A small business with $10 million in annual sales, for example, would therefore pay $200,000 in taxes and $200,000 would be distributed to employees through a profit-sharing plan. Employees working at the company would be motivated to ensure that all sales were reported because they would receive a portion of the sales revenue.

The proposed sales tax would be simple and straightforward. Businesses would still have the option, however, of staying with the current tax rate or switching to the new sales tax. Most businesses would choose the sales tax formula owing to its simplicity, which would result in great savings in overhead costs associated with legal and accounting fees in relation to tax filings and compliance. Eventually, the tax could also be adjusted based on the business sector or industry a company operated in. For example, wholesalers might end up paying a slightly lower rate than manufacturers. The process to simplify the tax system and dismantle all the hurdles and unnecessary rules and regulations that are hindering the ability of businesses to function efficiently will take time and are part of an ongoing process.

Over time, we could extend this simplified tax rate to a larger number of companies by gradually increasing the minimum number of employees required to participate from one hundred to as many as five hundred eventually. We could then assess the impact to the overall economy that this measure would have. Will it enhance productivity and economic growth? Will it reduce the government expenditures and administration related to taxation? Using this process, we would slowly change the tax system over an extended period while giving more and more workers the chance to participate in wealth creation.

Tax reform of this sort would be a win-win-win scenario. It would generate more income and long-term savings for employees, more profit for businesses, and more tax revenue for state and federal governments. Workers win. Businesses win. And governments win. The proposed tax would be simple to understand and easy to administer. There would be no guessing, no loopholes, and no gray areas. The administration overhead as well as all the accounting and legal fees associated with the current tax system would be dramatically reduced.

But we should not stop there. We should also move toward the elimination of personal income tax to be replaced instead by a flat consumption tax.

In the long run, I would envision only two tax systems: a corporate sales tax and a consumption tax that would apply to all goods purchased. The consumption tax would be anywhere between 18 and 22 percent, with the rate adjusted slightly up or down depending on the amount of revenue government needed in order to run a balanced budget. The flat-rate consumption tax would be much easier to administer and also much fairer since people buying luxury items and other high-priced goods would pay more tax. For example, assuming that the tax rate was 20 percent, a person buying a Chevrolet worth $20,000 would pay a consumption tax of $4,000, while a person buying a Mercedes-Benz worth $100,000 would pay $20,000 in tax.

Under this proposal, there would eventually be no tax on corporate profits and no tax on personal income—these taxes would be replaced in stages and over time by a simple straightforward sales tax for business and a consumption tax for individuals.

Lower tax revenues resulting from the elimination of income tax would be offset by the massive reduction in government spending associated with the filing and auditing of personal income tax. Whether it is business or government, the key watchword in today's world is efficiency, efficiency, efficiency.

We've allowed ourselves to get slowly sucked into a system that stifles individual initiative and smothers the key productive forces of society. And any society that stifles individuals in the pursuit of productivity, ingenuity, and creativity is a decaying society.

We spend more time and energy trying to place a ceiling on the upward mobility of our highest achievers than striving to raise the incomes of those who are at the bottom of the ladder. But the reality of today's global economy is that no nation or state can erect barriers to contain people with great talent or wealth.

That's why we must create the right tax environment so that our best people and most successful businesses remain here at home. Highly skilled people and investment capital are the backbone of a strong economy. We need to look at creating a tax system that would retain the very best people and investments—in other words, the brains and the money—that will create the new businesses of the future and generate new jobs. If we fail to retain the businesses and individuals that create products and services that can be exported around the world, our living standards will inevitably fall.

With the right tools, the right technologies, and the right time frame, even a desert can be made to bloom. A country is no different; we need to provide the incentives and create the environment that will allow our businesses to bloom and prosper.

Revamping the tax system along these lines would unleash an economic boom such as we haven't experienced since the end of the Second World War. It would put millions of people back to work. Most importantly, it would create the conditions necessary for enhanced productivity and wealth creation.

Making Corporate Taxation Fairer

America's current tax system provides incentives to destroy jobs.

One of the reasons for the steady decline in American manufacturing over the past decade is that the current tax system does not provide sufficient financial incentives to invest in the USA. On the contrary, America's current tax system provides incentives to destroy jobs. It allows American companies to reap greater financial rewards by laying off US workers and outsourcing production to foreign countries that have lower social, safety, and environmental standards than the USA.

Instead, we should remove incentives to invest abroad and create new incentives to invest here in America. An invest-in-America tax plan would encourage the return of offshore capital and penalize business investments outside the USA.

Here's what I propose:

First, in order to incentivize the return of offshore capital and stimulate economic growth in America, I would slash taxes on corporate profits currently sitting

Chapter 15

Making Corporate Taxation Fairer

"America's current tax system provides incentives to destroy jobs."

One of the reasons for the steady decline in American manufacturing over the past decade is that the current tax system does not provide sufficient financial incentives to invest in the USA. On the contrary, *America's current tax system provides incentives to destroy jobs*. It allows American companies to reap greater financial rewards by laying off US workers and outsourcing production to foreign countries that have lower social, safety, and environmental standards than the USA.

Instead, we should remove incentives to invest abroad and create new incentives to invest here in America. An invest-in-America tax plan would encourage the return of offshore capital and penalize business investments outside the USA.

Here's what I propose:

First, in order to incentivize the return of offshore capital and stimulate economic growth in America, I would slash taxes on corporate profits currently sitting offshore that get reinvested in the USA. As a result, companies that reinvested offshore funds would only pay a 10 percent tax on the profits brought back home, with the remaining 90 percent of the profits invested in product development, the purchase of new equipment and technology, and the construction of new manufacturing facilities and offices in the company's home country.

Second, in order to halt the flow of profits offshore and stem the loss of jobs to lower-cost regions, I propose establishing a 15 percent tax on all corporate funds invested outside of America by American-based corporations. It is unfair to American society and to American workers, whose hard work, ingenuity, and know-how contribute to the company's profitability, to have that company's corporate profits invested outside America.

Third, I would require American companies to be treated the same as American individuals when it comes to paying income tax. At present, American citizens are taxed on their worldwide income. However, the same policy should also apply to American corporations. All American corporations should be required to pay taxes on their worldwide corporate income, and this additional tax revenue would in turn be invested in renewing American's infrastructure and enhancing America's health and education systems.

Fourth, businesses would no longer be able to write off losses incurred in foreign countries against income earned in America—a destructive policy that has led to the exodus of millions of jobs, particularly within the manufacturing sector.

When large American corporations began sheltering profits overseas and taking other actions to avoid paying taxes in America, they were merely taking advantage of the current tax laws in America. They did not circumvent or break the law. But what they did was unfair to American workers and unfair to the country.

If we adopted the tax-reform measures outlined here, we would restore some fairness to the tax system in regard to corporations. These reforms would help put millions of blue-collar Americans back to work, pump billions of dollars back into the US economy, and create a spin-off effect throughout America's economy by spending money on new equipment and new buildings and by investing in new technologies and product development. Most importantly, these reforms would generate badly needed spending in America's real economy, which is built on the manufacture and export of products made in the USA and which is the backbone of the middle class.

Chapter 16

Restoring Balance to Politics

"The dilemma faced by Western democracies is that government must manage the country, but its decisions are driven primarily by political expediency. It's what I call the Achilles' heel of democracy."

It's hard to believe today that when George Washington became the first president of the United States, there were no political parties in America.

In his farewell address as president eight years later, Washington warned the young republic to avoid the pitfalls of partisan politics, saying it was the duty of American citizens to "discourage and restrain" the power of political parties.

He further felt that the entrenchment of political parties would ultimately lead to a tyranny or dictatorship of the parties, and he warned that the rise of parties over citizen representatives would ultimately "enfeeble" or weaken the running of the country.

Many believe that President Washington's prophetic warning has come to pass. Certainly, many Americans today feel that they live in a system where power and control rests with political parties rather than with the voters, a system where the politicians place their own self-interest and the interests of their parties ahead of the interests of the voters and the welfare of the country, with the result that the country is often paralyzed by partisan wrangling and political gridlock.

When the Founding Fathers created the American political system, with its various branches of government, they wisely built in a number of checks and balances. But what they did not envision—and what President Washington subsequently warned against—was the rise of party politics and the lack of an effective check on the growing power wielded by these political parties and the new class of professional politicians who represented their interests.

So taking the United States as an example, the question we face is the following: is it possible to modernize a system of government that has not changed in more than two hundred years? More importantly, how can we restore balance to democracy? How can we redemocratize our system of government and bring back the voice of the citizen in the governing of our national affairs? In other words, how can we ensure that the power of political parties is reined in and counterbalanced by the will of the people?

One way to overcome this would be to make government more responsive to the will of the people and better able to break political stalemates and deadlocks. In order to do that, I would propose excluding any political parties from being involved in the election of senators. Under my proposal, senators would become nonpartisan, duly elected citizen representatives. These "citizen" senators would continue to perform the same duties required of senators as spelled out in the US Constitution, and there would continue to be two elected senators from each state in the country. The one key difference is that the senators would be nonpartisan citizens, not bound by blind allegiance to a political party.

Any citizens wishing to run for the Senate would have to be a minimum of thirty years of age, as required by the Constitution, and would need to obtain a minimum of five hundred signatures from fellow citizens within their state endorsing his or her candidacy. Candidates would need to explain, in four hundred words or less, why they believe they could serve their constituents as a senator in the US Congress and would also have to fill out a formatted resume that reveals their place of birth, education, work experience, and financial net worth.

Finally, all candidates would have to produce a two- to three-minute video outlining why they want to serve as a citizen representative and what they could bring to their role that would benefit the country and their fellow citizens. The resume and videotaped message of each candidate would then be sent to the homes of all voters in the state.

There would be no advertising allowed on the part of the citizen representative candidates, and all election-related expenses would be covered by the government department in charge of administering federal elections. On Election Day, the two candidates with the highest vote totals would be elected as senators for their state.

By preventing partisan politics and the various party operations from becoming involved in the Senate elections, we would be able help break the ongoing deadlock that has frustrated voters and hobbled the ability of the US government to pass important legislation.

The Senate would become less a chamber for wealthy Americans who spend tens of millions of dollars to get elected and more a chamber of successful American citizens whose primary concern is the welfare of their country. The House of Representatives would still be comprised of politicians elected from one of the national parties, but we would strip away one layer of partisan representatives, creating more of a balance between the party-dominated House of Representatives and the nonpartisan Senate. Under this system, senators would be much more independent and no longer constrained by the straightjacket of party allegiance.

I've often said that **the primary mandate of a politician is to be elected or reelected**. As a result, the dilemma faced by Western democracies is that government must manage the country, but its decisions are driven primarily by political expediency. **It's what I call the Achilles' heel of democracy**.

Politicians should be expected to serve society rather than society serving their interests. As a result, all elected politicians should be restricted to serving no more than one term in office, after which they should go back into society and live with the laws they created. To further ensure that no individuals seeking public office are using their elected positions to enrich themselves, we should establish a system whereby all politicians undergo a thorough financial audit—both prior to entering public office and then one or two years after leaving public office to ensure that they have not received bribes and payments in exchange for political support.

However, I strongly believe that the introduction of citizen representatives would be the most effective way to help break both partisan gridlock and party dominance—two of the chief flaws in our party-dominated democracies. Citizen representatives would hold the balance of power, and their decisions would be based on the long-term social and economic interests of the country rather than being purely driven by political expediency or partisan interests.

President Washington was right when he warned that the will of the people could one day be subverted by the tyranny of political parties. The great statesman and parliamentarian Winston Churchill also argued for the creation of a nonpolitical body or chamber because he believed that elected politicians would always put their own short-term political interests ahead of the long-term economic interests of the country.

However, with citizen representatives, we would wrest back some measure of control from the professional political class that now runs the governments of most Western democracies. Citizen representatives would bring new voices and a different caliber of elected representative into the government decision-making process. They would more likely be small business owners and entrepreneurs and other accomplished citizens whose sole motivation would be to serve their country.

Citizen representatives would also bring a greater economic sensibility to bear on the issues at hand. They would help inject more common sense as well as the possibility of ridding the system of some of its most unsavory practices, including funding for special interest groups that are tacked onto budget bills by politicians using public tax dollars to curry favor with voters in their districts. Most importantly, citizen representatives would dismantle the stranglehold political parties have on modern-day politics.

The key tests for any proposals intended to reform our political system are the following: Is the proposal truly democratic? Is it viable? Can it be implemented without creating a major disruption to our current system? I believe the proposal to inject citizen representatives into our political process would meet all these criteria.

It's important that people constantly think about ways to improve the political system because government is ultimately the management team of our country, and the long-term success of the country is dependent on good management. I believe citizen representatives would be much more inclined to place the country's long-term national interests ahead of political considerations or partisan views. They would have one overriding goal or objective: the best interests of the country and its citizens.

I think America's Founding Father, if he were alive today, would approve.

Chapter 11

Balancing the Government Budget

I have often said that if you run a factory, it doesn't matter how productive the people on the factory floor are; if there is too much administration to run the business, will simply not be competitive. The same holds true for a country.

E very homeowner, businessperson, or farmer knows that you can't spend more money than you bring in or you will eventually go bankrupt. The only group that does not adhere to this fundamental law of economics is our politicians, who spend money the country does not have on various programs and special interests in order to get reelected.

In fact, governments in Western countries have been spending more revenue than they've been taking in for decades now. The result: enormous national debts that threaten to drag down national living standards.

At a time when countries are engaged in global economic warfare, it's not just businesses that need to become more efficient, so too do governments. The fact is, we're overtaxed, overregulated, and overgoverned. Politicians have created endless new government departments, agencies, and bureaus while citizens have sat back and allowed governments

151

Chapter 17

Balancing the Government Budget

"I have often said that if you run a factory, it doesn't matter how productive the people on the factory floor are if there is too much administration up top: the business will simply not be competitive. The same holds true for a country."

E very homeowner, businessperson, or farmer knows that you can't spend more money than you bring in or you will eventually go bankrupt. The only group that does not adhere to this fundamental law of economics is our politicians, who spend money the country does not have on various programs and special interests in order to get reelected.

In fact, governments in Western countries have been spending more revenue than they've been taking in for decades now. The result: enormous national debts that threaten to drag down national living standards.

At a time when countries are engaged in global economic warfare, it's not just businesses that need to become more efficient, so too do governments. **The fact is, we're overtaxed, overregulated, and overgoverned.** Politicians have created endless new government departments, agencies, and bureaus while citizens have sat back and allowed governments to grow unchecked for decades. We need to halt the buildup of government bureaucracy and regulations that are choking productivity.

The unchecked growth of government bureaucracy is one of the principal reasons government borrowing and spending is out of control. In most countries, the people are burdened with a government that continues to grow in size and scope, devouring a larger and larger portion of the national revenue. The end result is higher taxes on individuals and businesses and a less competitive economic environment. I often use a business analogy to illustrate the problem: if you run a factory, it doesn't matter how productive the workers on the factory floor are if there are too many white collars in the office up top. The business will not be competitive. The same principle holds true for a country.

Governments have the power to raise all the money they need through taxation. So why do governments borrow money? And why do banks not only willingly lend governments money but encourage them to borrow even more? The truth of the matter is this arrangement suits both governments and financial institutions. Banks prefer the safety and security of government bonds over riskier investments in private industry, and governments prefer spending borrowed money rather than raising taxes and risking the wrath of the voters.

As a result, politicians are driving us deeper and deeper into debt and printing more and more money. We are getting to the point very soon where we will never be able to repay the debts we owe. This will enslave and enfeeble future generations, shackling them with a huge debt. We are now being ruled by a new class system. This class is comprised of "politicrats"—my phrase for the new professional class of politicians and bureaucrats who work hand in glove to create more rules and regulations and an ever-expanding array of new government programs and then pass those rules and programs into law through legislation.

Back in the 1970s when computer firms were touting the benefits of computerization, businesses were told that computers would greatly enhance efficiency and eliminate an entire floor of employees who previously did the work that one computer could do. But today, fifty years later, everywhere you look, you see new office towers filled with more and more white-collar employees who spend hours and hours complying with government regulations and generating paper documents—all part of a massive data bureaucracy that is suffocating business.

We need to halt the growth of government bureaucracy and gradually reduce the size of the government through targeted cuts in government spending. This could be done without jeopardizing the environment, education, defense, or health by simply reducing government spending by 5 to 10 percent per year over a period of five years.

These cost-cutting actions would help reduce millions and millions in annual government spending, but the biggest savings would flow to businesses by unshackling them from all the costs and time eaten up by complying with unnecessary rules and regulations. The economic spin-off effect would be enormous.

One area of government spending that has grown out of control is the welfare system. The social safety net that Western democracies created following the Great Depression was designed to protect citizens from economic hardship and cushion individuals who fell through the cracks. Over time, that safety net has expanded and has become padded with more generous benefits.

But decades of welfare programs have created a growing class of people who are dependent on the government and who are idle most of their lives despite being educated and healthy. The key question with regard to social assistance is: Can we reduce poverty while preserving the dignity of people on welfare and also cut government expenditures at the same time? I believe we can.

I would propose that everyone requiring social assistance receive a government-issued credit card with a monthly maximum dollar amount along with minimum allocations for food, accommodation, and clothing. The card would guarantee that recipients could buy all their basic food needs, with minimum dollar amounts based on food requirements for individuals or families. The card could not be used to purchase nonessential items such as alcohol or lottery tickets. In essence, the card would ensure that people received nutritious food, affordable shelter, clothing, and other necessities of life.

At the same time, we should also take a closer look at whether or not the state needs to become more involved in interventions on behalf of children who are living in homes where there is physical, emotional, and mental abuse, neglect, malnourishment, and improper care. In an ideal society, all children would be raised by loving and caring parents. But the reality is that many are being raised in dysfunctional homes, with a parent or parents who are barely capable of looking after themselves because of drug and alcohol addiction or mental illness. Children growing up in this kind of environment are often destined to live the same sort of self-destructive life as their parents, dependent on government handouts for their entire lives. We should consider whether these abused and abandoned children ought to be raised in government-supported child-care homes, where they would have access to proper learning, nutrition, and physical education.

We've tried the current system of welfare for a number of generations now and it clearly is not working. On the contrary, we've created a system that breeds poverty from one generation to the next. Introducing a social assistance credit card will help make welfare what it was originally intended to be—temporary relief for those who have fallen on hard times and financial security for those who are unable to support themselves as a result of an accident or chronic illness.

Every citizen knows deep down in their bones that their country's economy is headed in the wrong direction. They know we are overgoverned, overregulated, and overtaxed. There is no escaping the consequences of runaway government spending and debt: one way or another, we will all have to pay for it. In the final analysis, we're destroying our children's and our grandchildren's futures.

It's high time that we faced up to our debt obligations and forced our political leaders to stop spending more than they take in. If we took immediate action— if we incrementally reined in government spending and gradually started shrinking the bureaucracy—we would begin to create the framework for long-term economic recovery and growth.

Chapter 18

Reducing Government Debt and Spending

"There is no escaping from the consequences of debt: one way or another, we will all have to pay for it. In the final analysis, we are destroying our children's and grandchildren's futures."

Take a look at the US National Debt Clock. At the time this book was being written, interest on the US national debt was growing at the staggering rate of $100 million per hour on top of more than $20 trillion in debt.

The buildup of debt throughout the Western world is a creeping sickness that weakens economies, devalues currencies, and deteriorates living standards. It's a sickness that is painless and virtually invisible at first. But by the time its cancerous effects are fully felt, it is often too late to recover and regain economic health. The debt payments grow larger and larger, and there comes a point when the debt-ravaged country is either no longer able to make its payments or other countries are no longer willing to lend it money, leading to an economic collapse.

For decades now, countries in the West have been spending more revenue than they have been taking in and have racked up massive debts in the process.

When individuals and businesses do this—when they spend more money than they take in—they inevitably go bankrupt. But countries, because they are able to print money, can postpone the process of going broke for a long time. And unlike personal or business bankruptcies, where the financial fallout is limited and contained, national bankruptcies affect every citizen and cause long-lasting, widespread damage.

Government debt is a growing cancer that will eat into our standard of living, devalue our assets, and limit the ability of future governments to provide the sort of benefits that citizens have grown accustomed to. The wealthy will be hurt the least since they will have the greatest number of opportunities to protect their assets and move their money to safe havens. The poor and those living on state welfare will get poorer, as the state will start cutting handouts because of falling revenues and a higher percentage of government spending on interest to finance the debt. But the ones hurt most of all will be the middle class. These are the people who will also have the most to lose, from personal retirement funds and state pensions, to devalued properties, higher tax burdens, and reduced buying power.

Most politicians know that spending is out of control, but they're unwilling to do anything that might loosen their grip on power. Basically, they're placing short-term political gains ahead of the long-term economic well-being of the nation, continually putting off the day when the bill will come due.

Some people have compared high-spending politicians to a parent who spoils their children by giving them everything they want, even if it's not good for them. While the comparison may be accurate, we cannot lay all the blame for our economic mismanagement at the feet of our politicians. It was us, after all, who elected them to enact the numerous programs and policies that were paid for with borrowed money.

Politicians will always use increased spending or spending on new programs as lures to attract voters. But it is ultimately the responsibility of voters to reject promises—and parties—that are not in the best long-term interests of the country. Government spending with borrowed money will ultimately cost the country a heavy toll in interest payments, higher taxes to cover those payments, and reduced spending in programs such as health care and education. There is a growing debt bubble building up, and that bubble will, sooner or later, burst.

Most people know based on their own lives that out-of-control spending has reduced their standard of living. If people take the past decade as an example, they know that the cost of many items has doubled while wages have remained stagnant or only risen by a small percentage. That means people are working harder now to maintain the same purchasing power and standard of living they enjoyed ten or twenty years ago. And the reason why their standard of living has declined is quite simple: the destructive combination of increased government debt payments and the buildup of government bureaucracy.

Voters need to handcuff the ability of governments to borrow money by pushing for balanced budget legislation to stop falling deeper into debt and to prevent politicians from spending more revenue than they collect in taxes. Governments, meanwhile, need to establish aggressive debt repayment programs with clear-cut targets in terms of repayment amounts and dates. And governments need to dial back spending. A simple 5 percent reduction in annual spending over a period of five years would reduce overall spending by 25 percent in just over one term in office—the equivalent of one-quarter of the budget.

We should also create a government task force entirely dedicated to reducing government bureaucracy and overhead. This task force would be guided by a volunteer advisory board comprised of experienced people in a wide range of industries, including business, medicine, education, agriculture, and the arts. The task force would examine the mountain of bureaucratic rules and regulations now governing nearly every aspect of our lives and critically examine each law with the aim of streamlining regulations and simplifying rules (for example, could we reduce regulations up to fifty pages in length down to five pages?)

Furthermore, we could incentivize bureaucrats to identify waste, duplication, and overlap. Just as in virtually every other aspect of life, people are driven and directed by rewards and penalties. We should establish substantial monetary incentives for government employees who identify areas where we can cut government waste and shrink the bureaucracy by eliminating or shrinking the size of various departments. As an example, bureaucrats who successfully identify areas that can be eliminated or reduced could receive a bonus equal to between 10 and 20 percent of the total money saved in annual costs.

As a society, we've gone far astray from the core principle that government should only provide a minimum number of essential services. Instead, we've embraced a philosophy that government should do everything—regardless of whether or not certain individuals can look after themselves and, increasingly, regardless of whether or not governments can afford to do so. And along the way, **I believe we have forgotten the truth that governments cannot give you anything unless they take it from you in the first place**, wasting a good portion of the tax money they collect in the process.

People are, to a great extent, a product of the system they live and work within. And if you have a system where too many people end up relying on the state for most of their needs, then there is less incentive to be more productive, to create businesses, and to generate wealth. More and more people begin to adopt a mind-set that the state will look after them. But I think that a growing number of people today in countries around the world are coming to the realization that you can't continuously milk the state. Eventually, there will come a point where there isn't any milk left—the state, and the taxpayer, will be sucked dry.

Chapter 19

Restoring Balance to Education

"Who's teaching the teachers?"

Our education system today is letting us down. It is no longer adequately preparing a larger number of students to become productive, engaged citizens with the know-how and skills needed to lead successful careers.

At its most fundamental level, education helps a society instill within its citizens the basic values of that society. Many of the values still held in great esteem in America—the values encompassed by our democratic rights and freedoms, our democratic system of government, and the free enterprise system that built our prosperity—are no longer taught and defended with the same passion and conviction.

I believe, therefore, that we need to establish a national values program that inspires our students by teaching them the core values that make America great. These values include our Bill of Rights, which guarantees, among other things, freedom of religion, freedom of speech, freedom of assembly, the right to a free and unfettered press, and the right to trial by jury.

These values also include our democratic system of government and the basic principles of democracy. But above and beyond that, there should also be some understanding about how wealth is created— the foundation of our Free Enterprise system—and how government taxes that wealth and re-distributes it. And there should be greater comprehension about how capitalism differs from socialism, an economic system that has spread throughout the world the past hundred years and which poses a direct threat to capitalism. Lastly, there should be greater instruction related to the importance of our natural environment and the ways in which it sustains life and produces the food we need to live healthy lives.

This national program should be taught from the first grade right through until the time that students graduate from high school, and it should be taught at every school in America. The national values program should be regarded as the glue that holds American society together, the heart and soul of American values, and the core of what America stands for.

We cannot forget that America was founded and built by people who hungered for freedom and opportunity, and those values are knit into the very fabric of the country. It is the reason why millions of people the world over still want to come to these shores and build a new life in America.

Our education system today has also become somewhat unbalanced. We need to restore a greater focus on physical fitness and health and athletic competition. We also need to place a much stronger emphasis in our schools on nutrition, particularly in the younger grades. And most of all, we need to return to a more balanced approach that stresses not only academic learning but also learning that is focused on technical skills and trades.

One of the first steps we need to take with regard to education is lowering costs and maximizing efficiencies in terms of public spending on educational facilities. The building and lands used to support education— the schools and schoolyards—are very expensive to maintain and could be much better utilized. The traditional summer break common throughout North America was established in the late nineteenth century, a time when most people lived on farms and farmers needed their children during the summer months to help bring in the harvest. That rationale obviously no longer applies today. Instead of giving children two months' vacation in the summer, it would be more economical if we adopted year-round schooling and gave children a number of periodic breaks over the course of the year—one in summer, one in fall, one in winter, and one in spring.

We need to do a much better job of exposing children to the trades. In essence, we're producing too many social scientists and too few plumbers and electricians. When I was fourteen years old, my mother took me by the hand and marched me down to the factory where she worked, and she asked the foreman to put me into a trade apprenticeship program. The practical skills I learned became the foundation for my future success in business.

Still to this day, European students who do not plan on going to study in university begin apprenticing in various trade programs at fourteen years of age. And while fourteen may be considered too young in North America, by the time a student reaches the age of sixteen, I believe they should be exposed to one or more various trades or industry jobs.

These jobs would include agriculture and food processing and packaging, wood and plastic fabrication, metal fabrication and basic metalworking, carpentry (as well as other building trades), and electronics. Students could spend half a year in any one trade and then rotate among a number of other trades over the next two years. Adopting this approach would help create the skilled technicians and tradespeople our country needs—everything from carpenters and mechanics to tailors and chefs.

The schools could work closely with industry to provide the learning associated with exposure to various trades. School districts could also become directly involved in providing some of this training. As an example, school districts could own and manage parcels of lands dedicated to agriculture. Various crops and vegetables would be grown, cultivated, and harvested on these lands, which would also contain greenhouses for the year-round growing of fruits and vegetables. Students from a number of different high schools within the district would be able to work on these plots of agricultural land to gain firsthand exposure to the food industry. At the same time, the food grown on these lands could be trucked to high school cafeterias to be used in the kitchen to make meals for the students.

The trades and industries that high school students were exposed to would be determined partly by the region in which the schools were located. So schools near maritime areas, for example, would be exposed to the fishing industry, while schools in more northern locales could be exposed to the forest industry or the natural resources industry. In general, we need to reduce the money and resources currently given to universities and direct those funds toward trade schools and technical learning, much like the land-grant universities in the USA established in the late 1800s with a strong focus on practical learning in fields such as agriculture, science, mechanical production, and engineering. These universities helped train the people who oversaw the great industrial revolution of the early twentieth century—a revolution that spawned the creation of whole new industries such as aviation and the automobile.

Students would be required to work for two to three years following high school graduation before pursuing studies at the university level. A university education should be seen as a privilege—not a right—and should not be pursued by everyone.

Requiring students to work before entering the halls of higher learning would prove tremendously beneficial to students because it would give them practical, hands-on experience and allow them to explore various career interests, test their skills, and discover what they really love to do and what they are good at doing. I've always been a big believer that when you like something, you will be good at what you do, and when you are good at something and you apply extra effort, you can be among the very best in your chosen field. But the real key for young people is to experiment by working in a few different jobs in order to get a feel for what they might like to do.

Requiring students to work for a few years would also be enormously beneficial to society. Many of the best managers in business started out working on the shop floor and then advanced their academic learning later in life once they were firmly established within a certain industry. Real learning—the kind that makes people successful—is often gained out in the field, in the factories, farms, and workplaces of a country.

Another area we ought to reexamine with regard to education is competition. Competition is so important in life, and it is one of the aspects of education we have let fade away. I believe we need to rekindle the competitive instinct by developing what I call "sports character."

Back in the late 1980s, when Mikhail Gorbachev was introducing a number of wide-ranging economic reforms in the former Soviet Union, the company that I built into one of the world's largest auto-parts makers became the very first manufacturer in North America to open a facility behind the Iron Curtain. On one of my visits there, a senior Communist official asked me to tour a number of Soviet automotive factories and assembly plants.

After seeing the various factories, filled with antiquated equipment and assembly lines that looked like they hadn't changed since the days of Henry Ford, the minister asked me what I thought. *"Not much,"* I replied. *"I don't think you can make quality cars at the right price and you can't make enough of them to satisfy the needs of your people."* And then I said, *"You know why your country always does so well at the Olympics? It's because you've got competition. If there was only one runner in a race, time wouldn't mean anything. Even a fat guy could win."*

Competition in its purest form is the essence of sports and athletic competition. **I believe our schools ought to develop sports character in our students by devoting more time to sports activities and other athletic endeavors.** As a result of a heightened focus on sports and athletics, we would expose our young people to the joys and rigors of competition, and this, in turn, would help them develop desirable social qualities such as leadership, determination, teamwork, and persistence.

The idea of making physical activity and athletic competition a key feature of youth education is not new—it goes back to the classical civilizations of ancient Greece and Rome. But it seems as if many countries have lost sight of the benefits that come with having a strong athletic component in the educational system. One exception to this trend is the USA.

I believe we need to look at the many nonacademic aspects of education that help develop well-adjusted citizens who will contribute to the social and economic well-being of society later in life. I **call this approach "lifestyle education"—the teaching of basic principles that will enable our young people to lead healthy, balanced, and productive lives**. As part of that focus on lifestyle education, we need to focus more on nutrition and healthy eating. All school children up to twelve years of age should be given one healthy meal every day. In addition, children should be taught about health and nutrition from the very earliest age.

Another key aspect of education reform is to reexamine how we train our teachers. In other words, we need to consider who's teaching the teachers? A large number of teachers in our high schools, colleges, and universities nowadays harbor a deep mistrust of business and, in some cases, have a strong anti-business bias. There also exists a perception among some of our teachers that if a business does well, it must be because it is exploiting its workers or engaged in unethical practices. However, teachers need to realize that making a profit is not a dirty word. This negative attitude dissuades young people from thinking about careers in business, especially as entrepreneurs.

That is why I believe it's important that our education system develops much closer ties with business. Students must be made aware of how important the economy is to the overall functioning of our society, and we need to place a much greater emphasis in our school system on the creation of wealth—the underpinning of our living standards. But greater involvement in our educational system on the part of business might dispel some of the negative perceptions students develop about business.

I believe that anyone wishing to become a teacher should be required to have a minimum of two years' work experience. Priority in hiring should be given to teachers with greater work experience since these teachers would be able to provide their students with a much greater degree of real-world insights, advice, and guidance.

We also need to ensure greater parental involvement in managing our education system. I moved back to Austria a number of years to help build a political movement and run in the federal elections taking place in 2013. After having lived in North America for so many decades, I was astonished that there were no school boards with democratically elected trustees in Austria and absolutely no parental input into the curriculum or the hiring of the teachers. The education system was controlled by unions and the curriculum was filled with socialist doctrines far removed from the basic values and principles of free enterprise and a free society.

Lastly, I feel that we need to do more in regard to teaching our young people how to become economically free. **I believe that most people desire personal freedom (the right to choose their own road to happiness) combined with economic freedom**—what might also be called financial independence. It astonishes me that we do not do more as a society to encourage economic freedom among individuals or encourage businesses to promote equity participation so that workers can become part owners in their places of employment.

At the same time, we should instill in our children, at the very youngest age, the importance of giving back to society. When I speak to students, I always say that they are fortunate that they've been given the opportunity to study and that students have the right to use the knowledge they've accumulated for their own personal benefit, but they should never forget that a portion of that knowledge and the wealth it generates should flow back to society.

Undergraduate university degree programs now typically last four years, which is far too long. These degree programs should be no more than three years in length. We need to reduce the amount of time during which young people are removed from the workforce in some of the most productive years of their careers. In general, we have far too many people in society who are not productive or who are idle for a great portion of their lives, preferring to subsist on welfare rather than becoming productive members of society.

And in much the same way the high schools need to be run more efficiently, public universities also need to be better utilized to maximize efficiency. To begin with, universities should be largely self-sufficient and government funding should only be used as seed money to develop new programs for new industries or to establish new highly specialized universities.

This would incentivize public universities to focus more on the needs of students than on the programs designed around the sometimes marginal areas of expertise belonging to academics. Students wishing to pursue a university education should pay for that learning themselves without any government subsidies or grants.

As I had indicated earlier in the chapter, by requiring students to work for two to three years before pursuing a university degree, they would enter higher learning with the means to pay for most of their education as well as a much better idea of what sort of careers they wanted to work in following graduation. Lastly, we should also examine the concept of tenure for academics. Although an age-old tradition dating back to the Middle Ages, we need to question whether or not tenure any longer serves a purpose in today's world.

Furthermore, we need to ask whether our colleges and universities can provide young people with the skills and knowledge they will need to develop innovative new products, technologies, and services. Will our centers of higher learning be able to produce the kinds of entrepreneurs and managers who can build successful businesses that create jobs and generate wealth? In other words, are universities and colleges giving our young people the skills and the knowledge they need to be competitive in today's global economy?

I believe that many of our universities have become too far removed from the realities of the competitive marketplace and global economy. Simply put, the world is spinning much too fast for these institutions. By the time a textbook is published, a great deal of the knowledge and theory in the book is already outdated. To make matters worse, you've got a large number of academics doing research that has absolutely no practical application. We are teaching our students about Communist theory while the rest of the world—including Communist China—focuses on creating wealth and improving living standards.

One solution is to establish smaller, more specialized universities as part of a coordinated public/private undertaking. For instance, we could create specialized universities that target learning and research in traditional industries, such as manufacturing or agriculture, or newer industries, such as biomedicine and space technology. By creating a number of these smaller, more agile, technology-based universities, we could generate some of the latest technological innovations, materials, processes, and production methods and thereby gain a competitive advantage in a number of industries. Both businesses and educational institutions should have a vital interest in establishing and participating in universities of this kind. In short, we need business and academia to come together to create new and applied knowledge for the benefit of society.

By reforming our educational system to incorporate some of the ideas I have outlined here, I believe we could help create citizens with the skills needed to prosper in the new global economy. It is the duty of the current generation to give our students the tools they need to create and compete and to open them up to the limitless possibilities that lie within their reach. If we can do that, then we will have a greater chance of ensuring our future prosperity.

Chapter 20

Restoring Balance to Health Care

"The key features of any system are competition and incentives. Without competition, and without incentives that reward the best and most efficient, no system—including health care— can provide quality service at a competitive price."

As a starting point, I believe that in a civilized society every person must have access to basic health care. The health care debate in some Western countries is becoming divided along lines of private care versus public care. But neither of these two systems works: in a completely private system, the poor cannot afford proper care, and in a completely public system, people do not have timely access to medical attention as a result of governments rationing health-care dollars and a limited number of health-care providers. I believe we can restore balance by creating a hybrid of the two systems or a system in which public and private health care coexist and work in unison.

The USA faces a particularly difficult dilemma. Spending on health care in America—both as a percentage of gross domestic product (GDP) and on a per capita basis—greatly exceeds spending in most other developed countries. Germany, for example, spends approximately 11 percent of its GDP on health care, as compared to around 17 percent in America, while per capita health-care spending in Germany is approximately $5,300 versus approximately $9,500 per person in the USA.

Yet despite the massive amounts of money the USA spends each year on health care (Medicare costs now eat up the same percentage of budget revenue as defense), a significant percentage of Americans remain uninsured. According to data from the National Health Interview Survey, conducted by the Census Bureau and the Centers for Disease Control and Prevention (CDC), approximately 10 percent of Americans—or roughly thirty million people—did not have health insurance in 2015, down from approximately 18 percent in 2013. To make matters worse, a significant percentage of Americans are driven into bankruptcy each year because of health-care costs.

Other obstacles that make health-care reform in the USA difficult include excessive litigation, which is driving up health insurance costs and driving some doctors and health-care facilities out of business, and the ability to purchase health-care insurance across state lines. The USA also needs to look at broadening its public health-care options, including the creation of more public and nonprofit hospitals.

And perhaps the greatest long-term fix to the US health-care problem is the issue of government policy with regard to the production and marketing of food products. Some of the many policy options available include: switching government subsidies for commodities such as corn and soy to fruits and vegetables or organic produce, banning junk food marketing to children, labelling genetically modified organisms (GMOs) in all food products, clearer and more detailed food labels, and prohibiting antibiotics and growth hormones in meats. The USA has one of the highest obesity rates in the world, and one of the main causes of skyrocketing health-care costs are the growing number of illnesses related to diets and the increasingly toxic food supply. Lastly, the USA needs to establish a Congressional Inquiry to pinpoint health-care problems and inefficiencies so they can be rooted out and addressed.

I believe it is the collective responsibility of society to ensure that every individual has access to health care and, furthermore, that we need to find new and innovative solutions to solve the problems in our current health-care system.

I see no reason why a public system and a private system could not coexist or why we could not create a hybrid system. To make it work, private health-care providers would need to make 10 percent of their billings available to the public at government-prescribed public rates. This would relieve the pressure on government funding and would foster greater competition among health-care practitioners without removing incentives to earn more. The key features of any system are competition and incentives. Without competition and without incentives that reward the best and most efficient, the health-care system will continue to experience higher costs and deteriorating quality.

As a way to deliver better health-care services at a lower cost, one solution I strongly advocate is pushing medical care into the workplace. By bringing health-care workers directly into the workplace to improve health-care access and services for employees and their families, we could reduce the health-care costs paid by employers, individuals, and the government.

Under my proposal, corporate-managed health-care services would be made available to employees and to their immediate family members (spouses, children, parents, and grandparents) and would be carried out with the consent of employees, who would remain free to seek medical care elsewhere if they wished. Employees would be required to take part in paid preventive health education in the workplace. Employees would also be involved in overseeing the management of the program through the appointment of advisory board members.

Lastly, all the stakeholders would get a cut of the savings associated with health-care efficiencies. Employees would share a portion of the savings in the form of a cash rebate, while the company would divide almost half of the savings among the various stakeholders involved. A portion would go to the doctors and medical staff in the form of an efficiency bonus to reward the more efficient delivery of health care services, and about 10 percent would go into a medical emergency account, which would essentially be a sort of rainy-day fund. Through my proposed corporate model for health-care delivery, I believe we could cut costs while improving services.

As part of the proposal, employees would take part in a program of preventive health care that would involve a minimum of ten hours per year of education and learning within the workplace for each employee. The preventive health-care program would stress the benefits of adopting healthy lifestyle choices and greater personal responsibility for individual health and wellness.

To me, the proposed health-care model is a total win-win proposition for all the stakeholders involved. Under the proposal, doctors would be relieved of administrative expenses, would be guaranteed a built-in clientele, and would be eligible for bonuses strictly tied to efficiency gains.

The company would have a healthier workforce and less absenteeism because of medical appointments. Employees would have more convenient service and the ability to earn health-care rebates. Society would benefit by delivering better health care at a much lower cost through a model that could be replicated by other large employers throughout the nation.

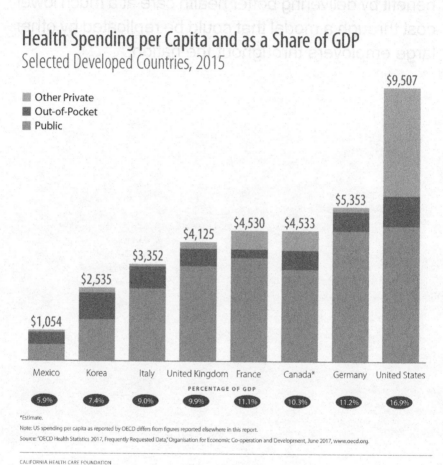

Health Spending per Capita and as a Share of GDP
Selected Developed Countries, 2015

- Other Private
- Out-of-Pocket
- Public

							$9,507

$1,054 $2,535 $3,352 $4,125 $4,530 $4,533 $5,353 $9,507

Mexico	Korea	Italy	United Kingdom	France	Canada*	Germany	United States

PERCENTAGE OF GDP

5.9% 7.4% 9.0% 9.9% 11.1% 10.3% 11.2% 16.9%

*Estimate.

Note: US spending per capita as reported by OECD differs from figures reported elsewhere in this report.

Source: "OECD Health Statistics 2017, Frequently Requested Data," Organisation for Economic Co-operation and Development, June 2017, www.oecd.org.

CALIFORNIA HEALTH CARE FOUNDATION

CHART SOURCE: California Health Care Almanac (September 2017), published by the California Health Care Foundation (http://www.chcf.org/almanac).

Chapter 21

Restoring Balance to Social Welfare

"If we accept as a basic principle that everyone in society must have access to health care, food, and shelter, then how can a society afford to look after those no one else will care for?"

W hen we look back in history to the days of primitive man and the tribes and chiefdoms of old, the family clan always looked after their sick, weak, and elderly.

But in today's society, particularly in the developed world, that is no longer the case. People are much more transient today—they move to where the jobs are, and in the process, families get split up and family members lose close contact. As a result, traditional family structures are becoming unravelled. This is why in North America, there is an explosion in demand for assisted senior care and a rise in the number of homeless people of all ages.

If we accept as a basic principle that everyone in society must have access to health care, food, and shelter, then how can a society afford to look after those no one else will care for?

I believe the optimal solution would be urban-based social service centers targeted at the 1 percent of society that require assistance from time to time—people ranging from teenagers to seniors and drug addicts to the homeless. These are people who simply fall through cracks or who suffer a severe setback that they cannot recover from, whether that setback is health-related or financial, such as bankruptcy or eviction.

When I look back on my early years in business, I was working up to seventy hours a week. One time, while delivering an order after working through the night, I fell asleep at the wheel and drove off the road into a ditch. On other occasions, I narrowly avoided having my hand cut or mangled by the machinery I was working on. If I had suffered an injury, I may have been unable to work and it might have cost me my business. Without the livelihood that my business provided, I may have been unable to support myself. But with a social service center, I would have had a roof over my head and some food while I recovered and got back on my feet again. In other words, the social service center would be a safety net for people who fall on hard times or become the victim of an unlucky circumstance.

I envision that a city with a population of one million people would have approximately ten social centers scattered throughout the metropolitan area. The shelters would be basic. Because land in urban areas is typically more expensive, each shelter would be about ten stories tall and would hold approximately one hundred people per floor, with each floor approximately ten thousand square feet in size. Approximately five floors would be reserved for single men, three floors for women and small children, and one floor for families. Each shelter would be located no more than a thirty-minute walk from where most people in the city used to live.

Each floor would have a common area that includes washrooms and showers (five per floor) as well as laundry areas with washers and dryers. The first floor would include a kitchen and a dining hall. The kitchen would serve basic nutritious foods such as soups, meat stews, pastas, and salads. The kitchen would also function as a drop-in center for people who are not staying at the shelter but who are hungry and in need of a meal. Also located on the first floor would be a medical office staffed by nurses and volunteer doctors. The medical services provided there would include treatments for wounds and minor cuts, scrapes and sprains, as well as equipment to do basic tests such as checking blood pressure. Serious illnesses or injuries would have to be treated at a nearby hospital.

Residents would receive clean bed linen every day. Each bed would be approximately 3 feet wide by 6 ½ feet long, with a footlocker at the end of the bed measuring approximately 3 feet long and 1 ½ feet wide for toiletries, books, and other personal items, and curtains between each bed that can be drawn in the evening for privacy. There would be a 4-foot gap between each of the beds and a 4-foot gap between each row of beds, with each floor containing approximately 10 rows of beds, measuring approximately 120 feet in length. In some instances, if space constraints are an issue, the beds could be placed together in quadrants of four with a five-foot-tall wooden partition in the shape of a plus sign separating each of the four beds.

The social housing centers would have a security staff, with consideration given to perhaps having the shelters run by military personnel in their first year of military training. The shelters would also be staffed by volunteers and student interns pursuing degrees in social service work.

Residents of the centers would be able to stay as long as they needed—no one would be forced to go live on the street. The centers would be built, funded, and maintained by the government, along the same lines as public housing. I believe the cost of building the service centers would, in the long run, be much cheaper than the haphazard, Band-Aid approach we are now using to deal with homelessness and inner-city poverty and addiction.

Social service centers should also be built in areas subject to natural disasters—everything from earthquakes and hurricanes to floods. These centers would play a great role in housing, feeding, and treating evacuees from various natural disasters, acts of terrorism or war, and disease epidemics. These centers would be able to shelter up to ten thousand people and would be operated by the army.

Back in 2005, I was sitting in a hotel room watching TV news reports of the worst natural disaster in US history. Hurricane Katrina caused flooding and damage that left close to one million people along the Gulf Coast homeless and in need of food and shelter. Most of the hardest hit victims were seniors and the very poor. Watching images of homeless and helpless people trying to flee New Orleans, I remembered my own upbringing in war-torn Austria, a time when I was poor and hungry. Those kinds of experiences are burned right into your soul.

I mobilized some senior executives at my company, and we put together an emergency rescue plan to move hundreds of evacuees by bus and plane to a horse training facility in West Palm Beach, Florida. The very next morning, a team from Magna was on the ground organizing supplies of food, water, and clothing and arranging transportation for the evacuees. Working with the US Army and Air Force, as well as the American Red Cross, we successfully evacuated 250 people.

More than 1,000 volunteers, doctors, nurses, and chefs were waiting at the Florida training facility to lend a helping hand as the New Orleans evacuees arrived. Among the evacuees were many families with small children, seniors, and disabled people. Some were wearing nothing more than shoes and a blanket. Many were carrying all their possessions in a garbage bag.

We wanted to find a way to help them rebuild their shattered lives. We bought a one thousand-acre parcel of land in Simmesport, Louisiana, north of Baton Rouge, and we started building a community from scratch, giving the Hurricane Katrina evacuees the opportunity for a fresh start and a new beginning.

Sometimes in life, some shelter and food—a place of temporary refuge—is all people need to get back on their feet again. I believe the social service centers described here would do just that for fellow citizens who have fallen on hard times.

Chapter 22

Revitalizing America's Inner Cities

"Revitalized neighborhoods, with partially community-owned urban farms as the focal point, would help to rejuvenate the pride and the spirit of the people living there by giving them a sense of purpose and a feeling of hope that their lives could be better."

Even though I've been involved in automotive manufacturing for more than fifty years, when people sometimes ask me what I do for a living, I usually say that I'm a farmer.

And that statement is essentially true. I've always had a passionate interest in farming, beginning with the first farm I bought soon after I started my business. Since then, I've purchased a number of farm properties, mainly for breeding and training racehorses. In the mid-1990s, I accumulated about ninety-five thousand acres of farmland in the Ocala region of Florida where today I raise grass-fed cattle and other animals.

Because I'm heavily involved nowadays in agriculture and food production, I think more often about the impact that food has in our lives, and I take great personal satisfaction in growing and raising healthy foods. I truly believe that healthy food production is the future. According to the US Department of Agriculture, approximately twenty-one million Americans are employed in the agriculture and food industry, and food production is a bigger industry than oil and gas, technology or automotive, where I spent most of my career.

In addition, I strongly believe that food production can be a sustainable, environmentally friendly generator of new jobs in America—not just in the farms and fields of the Midwest but in the very heart of our biggest cities. In short, I believe food production can be a solution to the grinding poverty and unemployment of our cities.

Let me explain. My company, the Stronach Group, is the largest racetrack owner in America, and one of the jewels in our portfolio of racetracks is Pimlico Race Course in Baltimore. Pimlico is the home of a Triple Crown thoroughbred horse race known as the Preakness, one of the most famous and storied sports brands in America. The Pimlico racetrack occupies approximately one hundred acres in the middle of the city, and surrounding the track are large pockets of poverty and crime, which often go hand in hand.

Although the poverty has grown over time and is unrelated to the operation of our racetrack, we are nevertheless neighbors and we want to play a role in improving conditions in the community where we operate. I think the key to everything in life is that when you have a problem, you need to seek out a way to solve the problem or eliminate it completely. That has certainly always been my nature. It's the way that I think and act. Life has been very good to me, and I am constantly thinking, *Can I give something back? Can I come up with ideas that would benefit society?*

So after a lot of consideration, we arrived at the following solution: because we only race at Pimlico a few days a year and because the track does not employ many people from the surrounding neighborhood, we have concluded that the track should be torn down and the racing moved to another one of our tracks, Laurel Park, which is closer to Washington, DC. And in place of Pimlico Race Course in Baltimore, we would like to establish one of the country's first urban farms as a role model for the revitalization of one of America's poorest urban neighborhoods.

Imagine if we were able to take the rundown inner-city neighborhoods of many cities—not just Baltimore—and turn them into pockets of urban farming that provided jobs, hope, and pride to the people who live there.

I believe we can. We could rebuild and reinvigorate these inner-city pockets of poverty by giving the residents an opportunity to gain meaningful employment and to restore pride and purpose in their communities.

The decay and poverty of many inner cities in the developed world is mind-boggling and grows worse by the year. Throwing money at this problem from time to time has clearly not halted the spread of poverty or improved the living standards of people in these neighborhoods. And ignoring the problem has allowed it to fester and spread. Simply tearing down the abandoned and rundown homes in the community and building new housing won't solve the problem, either, since it does not address the root cause of the poverty, namely, the lack of employment.

I would propose that we use urban farming as the vehicle to rebuild and rejuvenate these neighborhoods. We should consider building a prototype in three to five urban communities located in some of America's largest cities.

Here's how it would work:

Municipal governments, working in conjunction with state and federal authorities, would commence by identifying large parcels of inner-city land, typically around one hundred acres, with approximately three to five thousand residents. The dilapidated homes and apartments would be demolished and cleared in stages based on a master plan for the neighborhood revitalization project. Temporary housing would be provided for those residents whose homes were being rebuilt. These neighborhood revitalization projects would be financed by municipal bonds or debentures, and financing for the construction of the homes would be structured in such a way that the residents would have an opportunity to build equity in their housing units.

Of the hundred-acre parcel, approximately sixty acres would be dedicated to urban farming—the growing of food on land and in greenhouses. Another ten to twenty acres would be set aside for housing, and ten acres would be allocated to sports and recreation facilities, daycare centers, and schools (since half of the neighborhood population would be children). The remaining acres would be reserved for additional housing or retail space that the community could sell in order to pay back the municipal bonds that financed the community renewal project.

The schools in the community would have a strong emphasis on sports, nutrition, business, and community engagement. The revamped neighborhood would also include a small-scale social service center with one to two hundred beds and kitchens that would serve fresh, healthy, and nutritious meals.

About 10 percent of the population in the neighborhood would be older and retired individuals; 40 percent would be children between six and twelve years old; 20 percent would be children below the age of six; and the remaining 30 percent would be working-age adults. These adults, which would number around five hundred in total, would be employed growing and harvesting vegetables. The farms would also include on-site processing facilities for making various processed foods, such as jams, soups, and sauces from produce grown at the farm as well as from produce shipped in from nearby local growers who would form a partnership with the urban farm operation.

The farms could produce upwards of hundreds of thousands of pounds of vegetables per year. All the food would be chemical-free and GMO-free. The nutritious, high-quality produce grown would supply the food needs of the community and could be sold to other nearby regions on a for-profit basis.

The cost of doing this, in the long run, would be far less for society than maintaining the status quo. Residents would gain valuable experience working in the food production industry, particularly in the fast-expanding organic and natural food sector.

By creating this kind of environment with jobs and a focus on health and nutrition, most of the children would have the chance to grow up and become positive, productive members of society instead of becoming trapped in a continuous cycle of joblessness and poverty.

The rejuvenated neighborhoods, with community-owned urban farms as the focal point, would help to restore the pride and spirit of the people living there by giving them a sense of purpose and a feeling of hope that their lives could be better. Their neighborhoods would become an urban Garden of Eden, filled with fruit trees and fields of vegetables surrounding parkland and recreational facilities. The neighborhoods would be safe and inviting—the complete opposite of the urban blight that now characterizes most of these inner-city communities.

Residents in the community near our Pimlico Race Course would become part owners in our enterprise, receiving a 20 percent ownership in the business as well as a number of seats on the board of directors for our urban farming operation. As directors, they would also be involved in the strategic planning of the business. The resident-owners would also receive a portion of the annual profits earned by the company. The urban farms would work closely with local and state universities like the University of Maryland in order to utilize the most advanced, eco-friendly production methods and technologies for raising all-natural produce.

Is urban farming the best solution? I believe we need to try it, and I am personally willing to invest time and money into the effort. I believe the lands now occupied by our racetrack in downtown Baltimore could become the first test ground for what may be a simple but powerful and highly effective way to reinvigorate the dying neighborhoods of our inner cities.

I believe I have credibility with the local community and would like to spearhead the drive to use urban farming as a way to renew the neighborhood. About thirteen years ago, the automotive company I founded opened a technical training center in Park Heights, the rundown, crime-ridden neighborhood that sits next to Pimlico.

I met with some of the community leaders there to see if there was anything we could do to help the community. We got in a car and drove through the neighborhood. The best phrase I could find to describe it is that it looked like a war zone. One building in particular caught my attention: an abandoned elementary school. I asked whether or not we could take over the empty school because I wanted to turn it into one of the most modern technical training centers in the country. I believed that by giving people hope, by giving them some valuable training to land a good job, we could make a small contribution to tackling the poverty that had entrapped the residents of Park Heights.

As it turns out, one of our factory managers, who was working in Detroit at the time, had grown up in Park Heights just around the corner from where the empty school was located. He jumped at the chance to return to his old neighborhood and give teenagers there the same shot in that life that he had.

In January 2005, the Magna Baltimore Technical Training Center opened its doors to young African-American men and women living in the area. It was state of the art. The training program we launched in Baltimore turned unemployed youth living on the streets into skilled tradesmen earning a good middle-class wage. It helped change lives.

Turning our neglected inner-city neighborhoods into revitalized urban farming districts could do the same but on a much larger scale. Urban farming could provide meaningful jobs to countless thousands who currently have no prospect of finding work. It is my hope that we can create an oasis of urban farming in cities across America, turning broken-down and decrepit districts of urban decay into lively and thriving neighborhoods by restoring dignity to those communities so that the residents of those communities can say with great pride: come visit us and see what we have accomplished—come see one of the safest and most scenic city neighborhoods in all of America.

Restoring Balance to the Earth

We have to reverse the Earth's population growth and de-escalate the worldwide rise in population or our planet will no longer be sustainable.

In previous chapters, we noted how the Earth's air, water, and soil is increasingly becoming polluted and damaged with chemicals and millions of tons of waste generated by individuals and businesses.

We have created insecticides that kill pests on our crops and herbicides that destroy weeds so we can grow more food to feed the world. But that has resulted in poisoned water and dangerous declines in certain insect populations such as bees, which are a vital part of the world's ecosystem.

But equally as damaging to the Earth as these chemicals and toxins is uncontrolled population growth. The current rate of global population growth is not sustainable, and most of this population growth is taking place among the earth's poorest and least educated citizens, primarily in Africa and parts of Asia and South America.

The Earth can only sustain so much more pressure and demand on its resources before it begins to collapse in

Chapter 23

Restoring Balance to the Earth

"We have to reverse the Earth's population growth and deescalate the worldwide rise in population or our planet will no longer be sustainable."

I n previous chapters, we noted how the Earth's air, water, and soil is increasingly becoming polluted and damaged with chemicals and millions of tons of waste generated by individuals and businesses.

We have created insecticides that kill pests on our crops and herbicides that destroy weeds so we can grow more food to feed the world. But that has resulted in poisoned water and dangerous declines in certain insect populations such as bees, which are a vital part of the world's ecosystem.

But equally as damaging to the Earth as these chemicals and toxins is uncontrolled population growth. The current rate of global population growth is not sustainable, and most of this population growth is taking place among the earth's poorest and least educated citizens, primarily in Africa and parts of Asia and South America.

The Earth can only sustain so much more pressure and demand on its resources before it begins to collapse. In

2017, the Earth's population was approaching 8 billion. By the year 2200—only 180 years from now—the world's population will likely be more than 24 billion. By this point, the strain on the Earth will be so great that the most likely outcome will be the devastation of the Earth's natural resources and the onset of widespread disease and hunger. Some people, including the theoretical physicist Stephen Hawking, believe we do not have more than 100 years before the Earth is no longer able to sustain human life, at which point, we will face a mass extinction.

Either way, it is clear we are reaching a tipping point. We can no longer lie to ourselves or ignore the problem of overpopulation: it is one of the most serious issues facing our world. We need to urgently ask: can we do something about it? There is no perfect solution, but we need to take action now to save both humankind and our planet. Either we address the issue of overpopulation or nature will do it for us in the form of disease or hunger. One thing we can be assured of: nature's solution to the problem will be much more severe and swift.

However, I firmly believe that through education and planning, we can avoid these sorts of catastrophic scenarios. I also believe that measures to curb population growth would be very popular in many societies around the world. The birth rate is much higher in countries where the gap between the rich and poor is largest and where levels of education are the lowest. Over the long term, an enhanced and sustained education campaign can be effective in reducing the number of children that families have, and as certain societies become wealthier, the problem will remedy itself (as witnessed by developed countries that have much lower birth rates). In the near term, however, we need to come up with a plan.

One solution is to provide a one-time payment of $100 to $500 to any man or woman who voluntarily undergoes a sterilization procedure to prevent them from having children. In most societies, women bear the brunt of the burden when it comes to raising children. A worldwide program should be established to give women counselling and medical aid as well as a cash incentive to prevent pregnancy.

Under this program, women would voluntarily agree to have an operation to prevent further pregnancies after having given birth to two children. In addition, the program would include a global educational campaign to promote two-child families as the ideal family size.

The fact is, we are now reaching a crossroads in our evolution as a species. People have to become active participants in the solution to this problem. We have to reverse the Earth's population growth and deescalate the worldwide rise in population or our planet will no longer be sustainable. We will be placing ourselves on a path of growing poverty, disease, and environmental destruction. Solving this one challenge—the overpopulation of our planet—will do more to restore balance to our world than any other action we can take.

Chapter 24

Producing Healthy Food

"I'm a great believer in the old saying, 'You are what you eat.'"

I n the relentless pursuit of higher food yields and increased productivity, we have developed and dispersed a lot of chemicals in our air, water, and food that have ended up doing damage to the environment and to our own health.

Because we have introduced numerous pesticides, fertilizers, and other chemicals and medicines into our food supply, more and more people are eating a lot of unwanted chemicals in our foods. We are only now beginning to understand some of the health costs associated with industrialized food production, particularly in the meat industry, which has been using antibiotics, growth hormones, and genetically modified organisms or GMOs. But the use of GMOs is especially prevalent in the production of vegetables and grains ranging from corn and rice to tomatoes and beets. As a result, the health-care costs associated with treating illnesses linked to foods that have chemicals and other artificial ingredients continues to grow.

We need to begin identifying and banning the use of chemicals that are shown to be harmful to human health and the environment. In short, we must become stricter about what we allow to go into our packaged and processed foods as well as what goes into the production of our food—everything from fertilizers to pesticides and herbicides.

In tandem with stricter controls on the use of chemicals in our foods, we should also begin implementing nutritional education and awareness programs in our elementary schools at the very earliest grades. This will, over time, lead to enhanced health and greater avoidance of foods that are not chemical-free.

Some people believe that animal agriculture itself is to blame for much of the destruction to our environment. There is a lot of conflicting viewpoints on the part of scientists, environmentalists, and politicians regarding the benefits of farm animals to the environment, with some claiming that they contribute to global warming through increased carbon emissions, while others believe that the land devoted to animal agriculture could instead be used to produce more grain to feed a greater number of people.

Lost in this debate is the fact that animal farming is one of the greatest tools for enhancing the soil and our biodiversity. Growing different crops at different times returns vital nutrients to the soil and grazing animals such as cows and sheep is a natural way to help build the soil and restore dry and arid lands that were once subject to drought.

I'm a great believer in the old saying, "You are what you eat." The human body is a highly intricate organism and is susceptible to the detrimental effects produced by the expanding array of chemicals prevalent in our foods. When I was a kid, there were few children with food allergies. Now, it's the other way around; few children are allergy-free. More and more children are allergic to a wide variety of foods, everything from nuts and shellfish to peanuts and dairy products.

But there are other issues contributing to the rise of all-natural farming. People are increasingly concerned about the way that animals are raised. They want to know that the animals have been raised with care and have not been treated cruelly. At some of the large industrialized farming operations, the way that animals are raised, treated, and then slaughtered is barbaric. At these animal factories, animals are raised on massive feedlots and confined to small spaces, sometimes chained to posts, or locked in cages. They never see daylight. The conditions are atrocious and the animals undergo unspeakably cruel treatment.

Surely most people could agree that we should not treat animals this way. I believe that as a society, we should establish minimum standards with regard to the way animals are raised for food production. For example, every animal should have the right to a minimum amount of space in which to live as well as the right to be exposed to natural daylight.

In addition, there should be strict limits to how long an animal should be confined to a transport truck on its way to the processing facility or slaughterhouse. Any treatment that fell short of these minimum standards should be considered barbaric and should be met with strict penalties. Whatever specific standards we ultimately devise, we should be guided at all times by the principle of allowing animals to live as naturally as possible, free from cruelty, pain, or stress.

I have personally done a lot of soul-searching over the years in terms of the ethics of raising animals for food. A growing number of people are no longer eating meat for what they believe to be ethical reasons, namely, that we should not kill animals to obtain protein and other nutrients that are also available in nuts, grains, vegetables, and fruits.

I've often asked: is it right that we kill animals in order to eat meat? I believe they are creatures of God, just like us. They have a heart, a liver, and lungs. They have many of the same instincts that we do. They are conscious beings that have awareness and can sense their surroundings. And like us, they can feel pain and pleasure, joy and stress. Across the road from my company's European head office is a centuries-old church, and from time to time, I have lunch with the priest. Over a glass of wine, we have a lot of philosophical discussions, and one subject we clearly are in agreement on is that it is unethical to inflict pain and suffering on animals that are being raised for food.

I wonder as well if in a few hundred years from now people will still raise animals for food production. Will we reject the killing of animals for food on ethical grounds? Or will we simply lack the land, food, water, and other resources needed to raise animals? And if we will no longer raise domesticated animals such as cows, pigs, and chickens, where will these animals live? In protected sanctuaries? Or will they return to the wild where they will be forced to fight for their place within the ecosystem? Will the only meat-based protein available in the future be made in a laboratory? Whichever route we end up taking, it will be a long evolutionary process. The desire to hunt, kill, and eat meat is deeply ingrained in the human species and was a driving force in our own evolution. This instinctual urge will not be suppressed or swept away easily.

Either way, the production of food is one of the most crucial industries in the world today, and it will be even more important in the decades to come as the world's population grows. This will present an enormous challenge to produce good quality, healthy foods that the people of the world will need.

Pursuing World Peace

Countries and nations everywhere have a deep desire and longing for lasting peace with their neighbors. But what can the world do to try to curtail conflicts and avoid potential military confrontations that could lead to a world war?

One of the hard truths that history teaches us is that societies come and go. The world never stands still, and societies—no matter how great, how large, or how powerful—are all subject to the same unstoppable evolutionary process. We live during a time when several enormous industrial and military powers are engaged in global economic warfare, battling to stay ahead in a rapidly changing world.

China is the newest of these economic giants. When I go into a Walmart or other store nowadays, a great amount of all the products on the shelves have been manufactured in China. I've always been a big believer that a company should locate a portion of its manufacturing operations in the various markets where its products are sold. But many Western companies are only manufacturing in China so they can ship products back into their home markets in order to make higher profits. It is a formula for long-term economic decline.

Chapter 25

Pursuing World Peace

"Countries and nations everywhere have a deep desire and longing for lasting peace with their neighbors. But what can the world do to try to curtail conflicts and avoid potential military confrontations that could lead to a world war?"

One of the hard truths that history teaches us is that societies come and go. The world never stands still, and societies—no matter how great, how large, or how powerful—are all subject to the same unstoppable evolutionary process. We live during a time when several enormous industrial and military powers are engaged in global economic warfare, battling to stay ahead in a rapidly changing world.

China is the newest of these economic giants. When I go into a Walmart or other store nowadays, a great amount of all the products on the shelves have been manufactured in China. I've always been a big believer that a company should locate a portion of its manufacturing operations in the various markets where its products are sold. But many Western companies are only manufacturing in China so they can ship products back into their home markets in order to make higher profits. It is a formula for long-term economic decline.

China, on the other hand, has benefitted greatly from this trend in terms of economic growth and job creation. But as China grows wealthier, it will have to deal with the aspirations of its people, who will increasingly want greater individual freedom along with their improved standard of living. China is still very much finding its way in the world.

Russia is a rising economic superpower, one that will play an important role in Europe and America's future. Among all the world's emerging economic powerhouses, the Russians are not only closest to us in the Western world in terms of proximity, but they are also most like us in terms of their culture and mind-set. In short, they are natural trading partners and potential allies. But Russia is also one of the few countries in the world that can rival the USA in terms of military firepower and advanced weapons. Twenty years ago, it seemed that Russia was shedding its totalitarian past, but the country has since stalled along the road to democracy.

I fully understand that for both China and Russia the transition to becoming a robust democracy will be long and difficult. It's much like letting a tiger or wild bear that has been caged for a long time suddenly run free. But I think it's very important for the rest of the world that China and Russia take positive, tangible steps toward becoming true democracies. As it stands today, it's not clear which route these two countries will take.

And while China and Russia enjoy the prospect of strong economic growth for many years to come, America remains the world's foremost superpower. Even though America is going through a turbulent period, it is still the freest nation on earth, with the least amount of government interference. Moreover, Americans have a tremendous can-do attitude and a long track record of entrepreneurship and innovation that is unmatched. Because of all these reasons, I feel strongly that the USA will continue to be a global economic power for many years to come, and economic strength will ensure that America will also continue to enjoy unmatched military strength.

Countries and nations everywhere have a deep desire and longing for lasting peace with their neighbors. But what can the world do to try to curtail conflicts and avoid potential military confrontations that could lead to a world war? I believe one effective way to minimize tensions among the world's superpowers is to initiate improved dialogue between the leaders of the United States, China, and Russia, the world's three superpowers. This dialogue could be aided by ambassadors from the world of sports, business, and the arts. But of the three, I believe athletes would be the best suited to serve as ambassadors.

Here is why: athletes from the USA, Russia, and China compete against one another in global sporting events that range from the World Cup of soccer to the summer and winter Olympics. These athletes already serve as global ambassadors of respect, friendship, and fair play. It's not surprising, therefore, that the International Olympic Committee, which was founded more than a century ago, was built on the belief that sport could make a positive contribution to world peace and what it believed was the "harmonious development of humankind."

These athletic ambassadors have tremendous character and integrity and have competed against one another at the very highest levels. They also have a deep mutual respect and admiration for one another. That is why I believe they would be the ideal ambassadors to initiate dialogues and discussions designed to ensure that we could resolve disputes diplomatically and without resorting to military force. In fact, there is a long and proud tradition of using athletes as ambassadors to resolve political disputes.

The ongoing dialogues between the three superpowers would be televised across the world; would involve high-ranking government officials as well as athletes, businesspeople, and environmentalists; and would take place on a monthly basis, with the site of these dialogues rotating between Washington, Moscow, and Beijing.

The dialogues would be a frank and public display of the hopes, fears, and aspirations of the people from these three superpowers, which in turn would demonstrate that the countries have far greater similarities than differences, which are often the source of tension and conflict.

One of the key challenges confronting the world going forward is figuring out what we must do to avoid global conflict and war. In order to ensure that the world's superpowers remain engaged in dialogue and discussion, we should pursue every avenue possible. We need to seek open dialogue between nations, but that dialogue is too important to be left solely to politicians.

Chapter 26

The Transformation of Work

"Jobs are the greatest currency of the twenty-first century."

B ack in the 1980s, the small tool-and-die shop I started in a rented garage three decades earlier had grown into the world's most diversified automotive-parts maker. We made everything from the bumper and the hood to door latches, transmission pulleys, and seat tracks. But even back then, it was clear that automation and robotics were beginning to replace workers. More and more of the welding on steel parts was being done by robots. When I first started, those tasks would have been done by hand by a skilled tradesman. Robots were also being used more and more to pick up and move large, heavy components on the production line.

Fifty years ago, robots and artificial intelligence were the stuff of science fiction. But today, they are increasingly part of our society, particularly in the workplace, where robotics and automation are displacing a growing number of workers. In the decade ahead, everything from self-driving transportation trucks to elder-care robots will cause the loss of millions of jobs.

More recently, we are seeing the rise of Artificial Intelligence (AI) technology, which will likewise displace a great many jobs, although most of these will be white-collar jobs. But who are the beneficiaries of these new technologies? And what will we do with the millions of people who will inevitably lose their jobs to the adoption of these new technologies?

The fact is, in the future, there will be very few people who make products in developed countries, in much the same way that only a tiny fraction of the population today works in agriculture, whereas in 1850, the majority of people living in North America worked in farming and food production.

So where will the jobs of the future come from?

The expanding service industry will comprise a much greater portion of the economy in the future— everything from health care and specialized food services to personal fitness. And it is within the service sector where many of the workers displaced by robotics and automation will find new work. Many of these jobs, however, will be low-skill, low-wage, and part-time in nature. They will clearly not provide the standard of living that citizens in the West have become accustomed to. Even many of the higher-paying service jobs such as financial services, engineering, and communications are increasingly being outsourced to workers in India and the Philippines.

The area of the economy that will grow most rapidly in the decade ahead will be those products, technologies, and services that enhance our quality of life. These products and services will include biomedical advances designed to prolong our lives and make us healthier. I believe the agriculture industry will also grow in importance in the decades ahead because of a greater focus on food safety and quality. Many of the jobs connected with the industry will be high-wage, knowledge-intensive jobs involved in the application of scientific research for the purpose of developing new crops and natural, sustainable foods.

However, despite the fact service jobs will outnumber manufacturing jobs in the developed world, I believe that we in the West should reverse the enormous trend toward financial engineering and services and, instead, focus once again on our once-proud manufacturing traditions.

Our economies grew strong by making the kind of products the rest of the world wanted—products that improved lives and helped generate new wealth. It is only through focusing once again on making things—innovative new products that combine the very best in our knowledge of new materials and technologies with our most advanced engineering and design skills—that we will be able to create the jobs of the future.

With the rapid growth in robotics and full automation in manufacturing, we need to put in place certain measures to ensure that manufacturing is not controlled by one or two robotics companies. Monopolies, whether they are private sector– or state-owned such as airports, are always bad for society. One way to prevent monopolies, particularly with regard to robotics, is to enact a law that no company can have more than 40 percent market share in this critical industry, and moreover, that there must be a minimum of three companies supplying the manufacturing industry.

To strengthen this law even more, we could restrict market share to 30 percent, thereby ensuring a minimum of four competitors in this vital segment of the economy. This anti-monopoly measure should eventually apply to all industries from packaged goods and phones to computers and automobiles.

There was a time, during the 1970s and 1980s, when computers and automation were changing the way we worked, that some futurists and economists predicted "the end of work." Many of these people claimed that by the year 2030, most people would no longer need to work, as robots and automation would perform virtually all the jobs we used to do while incomes would rise because of the wealth these new technologies generated.

It hasn't quite turned out the way—at least not for the majority of people. If anything, people who have jobs are working longer than ever and seeing their incomes decline. But undeniably, many jobs are beginning to disappear because of technological advances, and these job losses have dragged down the living standards of a growing number of people. When I was chairman of the company I founded, Magna International, I would regularly be courted by states and jurisdictions around the world that wanted our company to locate production facilities there. It made me realize that jobs are the greatest currency of the twenty-first century.

One concept that is gaining popularity is "universal basic income," sometimes referred to as guaranteed annual income. The universal basic income would guarantee every citizen a predetermined minimum annual income regardless of age, wealth, or employment. I strongly believe that the establishment of a universal basic income would do more harm to society in the long run.

If we go down this road, I foresee two likely outcomes, both of which will be detrimental to the long-term health of society and the economy. The first outcome is that we will create a whole new class within society composed of individuals who are content to sit back and remain idle, happy to live on the minimum subsistence handed to them by the state. The end result is that, over time, the built-in human drive to be self-sufficient would gradually weaken and fade, and we would produce a growing segment of the population that is totally reliant on the state.

The second outcome would be an increase in the number of government bureaucrats, administrators, and technocrats required to oversee and administer the universal basic income program, which would end up bloating the bureaucracy even more.

Regardless of whether automation, robotics, and artificial intelligence one day replace much of what has much been the work done by humans, humans will still always want to work. There will always be people who want to create new products or technologies or works of art, people who will want to take what currently exists and make it better, faster, stronger.

It is impossible to stifle the human urge to create and produce. An ideal society would foster this imaginative aspect of human nature, whereas any society that seeks to suppress individuals in the pursuit of productivity, ingenuity, and creativity is a decaying society that is doomed to eventually fail.

Chapter 27

Harnessing the Human Instinct of Greed

"Any society that stifles its citizens in the pursuit of greater creativity, productivity, and innovation is a dying society."

Greed is a basic instinct for the survival of the human species. We are all born with this instinct—it is deeply embedded into each and every one of us.

Greed can be a very destructive force. But when properly harnessed, it can also spur individuals and societies to achieve incredible advances in commerce, art, and science. I have always maintained that any society that stifles its citizens in the pursuit of greater creativity, productivity, and innovation is a dying society.

As people, it is within our nature to want to do better— to hustle and work hard in order get better clothes, cars, or homes. This natural desire to accumulate more is not only a selfish impulse. People also amass wealth because they want to pass some of that wealth onto their children so that they can have a better life.

I believe that success in life can only be measured by the degree of happiness you reach. But at the same time, I also believe—especially based on my own personal experience—that it's a lot easier to be happy if you have money.

So if we attempt to repress the human instinct of greed, we will also remove one of the primal forces that drives human progress. Whenever governments adopt punitively high rates of taxation on wealthy and highly successful individuals, then it ultimately leads to a decline in productivity and innovation.

We need to focus on finding ways to lift people out of poverty. And we need to be careful that we don't limit or shut off the avenues that allow people to get ahead and make a better life for themselves and their families. We should never smother the human impulse to do better and to want more. Even though some people have to clean the sewers, as a society, we must always ensure that we never screw the sewer covers on so tightly that someone can't climb out and perhaps one day hold the highest office in the land or own the company that builds the sewers.

At the same time, we cannot pull down those among us who are trying to rise higher and reach the very top of their respective fields, whether it be in business, science, academia, or the arts. The desire to be the best and to pursue excellence is a powerful human desire. When our children or grandchildren play sports, they often dream of one day becoming a world champion or a gold medal winner. And with success often comes financial reward, a natural by-product of excellence in any endeavour. Our goal as a society should be to help make those individual dreams come true by eliminating obstacles and moving out of the way of those who are trying to climb higher.

The most highly skilled and creative people in the fields of science, art, sports, and business—people whose talents are in great demand—are able to live and work anywhere in the world. We can't blame highly skilled people for moving to countries or jurisdictions where they can make more money. The same is true of businesses. The reality of today's global economy is that no nation or state can erect barriers to contain people with great talent or wealth. It's critical, therefore, that we don't stifle or drive away the entrepreneurs and inventors who are the engines of new wealth creation.

Instead of heavily taxing the wealthiest members of society, I believe that a fairer and more productive solution would be to give high-income earners the option of a once-in-a-lifetime tax on net assets worth more than $5 million. In lieu of an estate tax, these individuals would be given the option of instead donating 10 percent of the value of their estate to a number of government-approved charities and nonprofit organizations focused on helping young people.

Individuals would be able to direct their estate money all at once or in installments over a period of five years. So if their estate was worth $10 million, they could pay out the 10 percent, or $1 million, in amounts totalling $200,000 per year for five years, or they could pay out the $1 million all at once. The choice would be theirs.

The real benefit of this approach is that it keeps tax dollars out of the hands of governments that are already too big and bloated and puts that money instead into groups that are helping to make young people healthy, well-adjusted, and productive citizens. Youth are the future of any society, and the more money we can direct toward their development, training, and education, the stronger our society would be.

Greed has an enormous bearing on a society and its citizens. It can be a force for both good and bad. Too much greed is often harmful. But some greed is good, even necessary. Without it, we wouldn't exist. The instinct of greed is a perfect illustration of how nature sometimes contains within itself two conflicting and opposite forces, and these forces in turn are forever seeking balance and equilibrium.

And although greed can be checked, it can never be suppressed. The unstoppable human urge to do better and acquire more is what propels our society forward, which is why it's important that we do not penalize those who utilize their skills and talents to accumulate wealth.

Giving Back: Making a Contribution to Society

"From time to time, all of us should take a moment to look in the mirror and ask ourselves how we might be able to serve society."

Around the time that my company reached the billion-dollar sales mark in the mid-1980s, I was heavily involved in helping various charities, hospitals, and universities, and I served as a director on the boards of numerous nonprofit organizations.

One year I was invited to take part in a university panel discussion in the United States on leadership. Joining me on the panel were senior businesspeople and government leaders. The purpose of the seminar was to see if we could create a curriculum in regard to public leadership.

When it came my turn to speak, I asked the audience the following: "Leadership is vital, but leadership for what? To lead a society into war? Leadership to create a new religious sect? I believe that when we talk about public leadership, the first question we need to ask is this: what would constitute an ideal society?"

I then went on to say that we have to understand that a society is made up of individuals, and we should therefore try to understand what are the hopes, dreams, and aspirations of individuals. As I indicated earlier, I firmly believe that people crave individual freedom above all else.

In simple terms, that means that each person wants to choose his or her own road to happiness. But individual freedom doesn't mean much to an inner city kid in Detroit or teenagers in some of the poorest neighborhoods in Calcutta or Rio de Janeiro. It just means you're free to be hungry and free to be poor.

The fact is, people also have dreams and hopes to be economically free. Even though we in the West live in highly advanced and prosperous societies, it is a shame that only 5 to 10 percent of the people are economically free.

So the message that I continually try to communicate is this: what can we as a society do to fulfill the hopes and dreams of individuals everywhere? In other words, what must we do to ensure greater freedom and prosperity for all people? I believe the leaders who can best answer these questions are the leaders that people will increasingly turn to in the years to come.

The other key question we should ask ourselves is: How do we as a society define success? Is success about creating something—a product or service or idea that makes a lot of profits? Or can success also be about developing something that benefits society?

I believe people everywhere, regardless of income or education or religious background, should try to give back and create a better life and better world for their fellow citizens.

Our first and foremost thought should be: can we make a contribution so that people have a better, more fair, and balanced life because that is what each of us would like for ourselves.

We should also teach our children that we can all give back to society and that there are many ways to give. For example, we could give back by donating our time to perform volunteer social work or helping the elderly. For others, who have less time and more money, they can donate some of their money to various causes and projects that advance medicine or alleviate poverty.

Our children should also spend a few minutes each day at school in silent reflection. This would be a moment where they could ask: Can I do something good for society today? And this moment of reflection could be a guideline for all of us, young and old, so that each day we think about something that we could do to benefit our fellow humans and the society we live in.

One of the great dangers we as a society need to be on guard against is when citizens, especially our young people, become pacified to the point where no one any longer cares about trying to improve society because everyone considers that to be the sole responsibility of the state.

Back in the 1970s and 1980s, I volunteered for a charitable organization known as Big Brothers. The mandate of Big Brothers is to match adult male volunteers with boys who have no father in order to give the boys a role model while also offering them support, encouragement, and guidance.

As a Big Brother, I would take my Little Brother to sporting events or sometimes to the office where I worked. I enjoyed the time I spent with him; it made my heart feel good knowing that I might be a positive influence in the life of my Little Brother. Like any volunteer, I gladly and freely gave my time and energy, without any expectation of payment or reward. That is the essence of the volunteer spirit. I used to joke that if the Big Brother organization were run by the government, you might end up with a bureaucrat who would say: *"The pay's great, but I hate spending time with the little brat."*

These experiences I've gained over the years working for charities and nonprofit organizations such as hospitals and universities have given me valuable insight into the many needs and issues that exist in society. Not only do businesses have a responsibility to support the social fabric, but so too do individual citizens, especially those among us who are more fortunate and who have the means and opportunity to give back to society. From time to time, all of us should take a moment to look in the mirror and ask ourselves how we might be able to serve society.

Chapter 23

Unleashing a Revolution of the Mind

"I believe that all of us today are literally writing the future of humanity. Will it be paradise on earth or will it be a nightmarish world marked by war, hunger, disease, and poverty?"

We are entering a perilous time in human history, a time when a wrong turn could lead to our ruin and our eventual demise. However, we have within us the ability to change the world—not through the type of violent revolutions that have marked human history over the centuries but through a peaceful revolution of the mind.

The human spirit possesses incredible energy and willpower that could lead us to an ideal society. Within the course of the next century, humankind should have attained a new plateau—a world free from hunger, poverty, and warfare—a world filled with abundance and harmony.

I've spent many years thinking about this book. The further you look back into history, and the more you look ahead to the future, the more philosophical you become in writing this book. I am drawing on my many decades of experience in the hope that I can make a small contribution to make our world a better place. I

Chapter 29

Unleashing a Revolution of the Mind

"I believe that all of us today are literally writing the future of humanity. Will it be paradise on earth or will it be a nightmarish world marked by war, hunger, disease, and poverty?"

We are entering a perilous time in human history, a time when a wrong turn could lead to our ruin and our eventual demise. However, we have within us the ability to change the world—not through the type of violent revolutions that have marked human history over the centuries but through a peaceful revolution of the mind.

The human spirit possesses incredible energy and willpower that could lead us to an ideal society. Within the course of the next century, humankind should have attained a new plateau—a world free from hunger, poverty, and warfare, a world filled with abundance and harmony.

I've spent many years thinking about this book. The further you look back into history, and the more you look ahead to the future, the more philosophical you become. In writing this book, I am drawing on my many decades of experience in the hope that I can make a small contribution to make our world a better place. I hope that people who share these concerns, people of goodwill and compassion, will take up this cause and contribute to the search for the ideal society that will benefit humankind.

I believe that all of us today are literally writing the future of humanity. Will it be paradise on earth or will it be a nightmarish world marked by war, hunger, disease, and poverty?

In these many chapters, we have certainly concluded that one of the keys to an ideal society is the search for balance. It is one of the guiding principles of the universe.

It is my strongly held belief that humanity must embrace a symbolic goodness—a concept of what is good, whether it be God or some other spiritual force. That belief can inspire us on our journey forward.

But at the same, I also know that we humans are born with the instinct of greed. It is embedded into each and everyone us for the survival of the human species. And because of it, we carry within ourselves the seeds of our own destruction.

In stories and in the movies, the "good guys" almost always win. It's a desire that is deeply rooted within the human heart and soul, a storyline we all want to believe in. But unfortunately in life, the "good guys" don't always win, and good does not always vanquish evil. And that is one of the messages of this book. Are we on the right path? Or are we headed to disaster and destruction?

I included the *Pegasus and Dragon* monument in my book because of the symbolism it contains. The monument pays homage to the courage, speed, and power of the horse, which has made great contributions to human civilization throughout history. But *Pegasus and Dragon* is also part-fable and part-fantasy, within which lie universal truths. *Pegasus and Dragon* symbolizes far deeper themes that illuminate the human condition—including the search for balance and the eternal battle between good and evil, light and darkness.

The monument is really the embodiment of these two eternal forces forever entwined in conflict and combat. The human urge to uphold what is good and right and beautiful, to overcome tyranny and oppression—these are the age-old longings that guide us on our journey toward the ideal society.